The Angler's Mail guide to
Basic Sea Fishing

The Angler's Mail guide to

Basic
Sea Fishing

Consultant editors: John Ingham & Roy Westwood

Hamlyn
London · New York · Sydney · Toronto

Contributors

Bob Gledhill
John Holden
Mike Millman
Russ Symons
Alwyne Wheeler

Illustrations by Tony Whieldon

Identification illustrations on
pages 93-115 by Peter Stebbing

Title spread The necessity of fishing the tide at the optimum moment
often involves the shore angler in late evening or early morning vigils,
as here at sunset on a beach in North Cornwall.

This page The British record conger of 109 lb 6 oz caught from a wreck
on the south coast of England.

Identification illustrations © 1978 Peter Stebbing

Published by The Hamlyn Publishing Group Limited
London · New York · Sydney · Toronto
Astronaut House, Feltham, Middlesex, England.

Copyright © The Hamlyn Publishing Group Limited 1981
ISBN 0 600 35385 0

Reprinted 1983

Phototypeset by Photocomp Ltd., Birmingham, England.
Printed in Spain.

Contents

Introduction

The history of modern sea fishing goes back a long way. By the 1920s it was becoming a major sport and even railway companies, alive to the opportunities of transporting enthusiasts to various parts of Britain, published guide books containing haunts and hints for anglers.

Today sea angling is the fastest-growing of all the many branches of sport fishing. That is the verdict of a recent official national survey. The reason is not hard to understand. With a few exceptions an angler can cast a line anywhere from the coastline at no cost beyond that of getting to a desired spot. Gone are the days when shore angling was regarded as a summer sport. It is now a year-round activity with only the species changing.

Shore and boat fishing is no longer a 'chuck and chance it' affair. It has become a science with the angler giving deep thought to what species may be expected for the time of the year, the type of ground most likely to yield a catch, the choice of correct tackle and the right bait for the species in mind.

'How do I start?' is a question often asked by would-be anglers. The simple answer is join a bona-fide club. There are well over a thousand in Britain, many based miles from the sea. Contact with other enthusiasts is often a short-cut to success. Organised club outings give the opportunity to visit marks that would otherwise probably remain unknown for some time and techniques used by experienced anglers are revealed. Most sea angling clubs are members of the National Federation of Sea Anglers, which in turn is sub-divided into divisions.

The design of fishing tackle has come a long way in the last 20 years. Major manufacturers now produce rods that are absolutely right for the many different aspects of boat and shorefishing. They range in price from a modest tenner for hollow-glass to many hundreds of pounds if tastes run to high technology carbon fibre. Reels are a masterpiece of engineering and usually give years of silky, trouble-free service. Modern tackle catalogues are more than a collection of pages showing pictures of equipment and their prices. A great deal of information is given on the type of fishing for which specified rods and reels are suitable.

It is always good policy to buy the best you can afford. Specialist tackle retailers carry a bewildering range of rods, reels, lines and a thousand other items. More often than not the men behind the counter are enthusiasts with years of practical fishing experience. Newcomers should not hesitate to say if they are just starting in the sport. A great deal more knowledge on the varying techniques of shore and boat fishing, and new trends, can be found in lively articles published every week in *Angler's Mail*.

Approximately 100 species are listed among British Records but, to all intents and purposes, only a score come frequently within range of shore anglers. Boat fishing enthusiasts have rather more to challenge them but the total is not considerably greater.

When considering the species to go for, a newcomer must take into account the time of year. Fish movement and migration has a predictable pattern but varies in different parts of the country. In the winter, East Coast beach anglers are seeking cod and whiting but those on the South Coast, and to a greater extent the West Country, are engaged principally with flounder in the tidal rivers. Cornwall's north coast is a hotspot for codling, whiting and spurdog, while similar fishing is enjoyed by enthusiasts on the great shingle beaches of Dorset.

In the summer, bass, mackerel, garfish, wrasse and mullet hunt inshore and in some places there are black bream to catch. Several varieties of ray may be

found, among them thornback which appear in estuaries and tidal rivers in the early spring. From September, small-eyed ray are the quarry of many enthusiasts who fish at night.

The conger is an all-year fish for shore anglers and great sport can be had from piers, harbour walls and tidal rivers. Another hard-fighting species is the coal-fish, which has been taken by shore anglers to a weight of 18 lb. Winter is also the time chosen by outsize pollack to hunt close to land. Hardly a winter goes by without at least a dozen fish weighing well into double figures being recorded. It is, however, primarily a fish of the summer in most areas.

The easiest fish for a beginner include

The rewards of summer fishing – a warm day and a gentle Atlantic swell, ideal for bass and flounder.

wrasse, mackerel, garfish and dogfish. Thornback ray are also a worthwhile proposition.

On the boat fishing scene, 'wrecking' is at its very best between November and late February, when pollack, ling and coalfish group together. It is a time for record-breaking as the females are heavy with spawn and the increase in weight is dramatic. For example, a female pollack of say 16 lb during the summer will be carrying at least 6 lb of roe by early February.

Reef and rough ground fishing in winter is really nothing to shout about, but attention given to flat muddy and shingle bottoms will result in excellent catches of whiting and cod. In the spring, the same type of ground and the great sandbank areas of the English Channel, such as Varne, Shambles and Skerries, are invaded by plaice and dabs. By mid-May turbot and brill have joined them and the same ground will be quartered by large bass plus red and black bream. The reef angler begins to find top action in June, when pollack, ling, haddock and bream arrive in large numbers. There are exceptions but the seasonal chart gives a fairly accurate picture of which species to expect at certain times of year.

The newcomer to rock fishing should have no difficulty catching shoal species, such as whiting, pouting, red bream and medium-weight pollack when he is over the right type of ground. The outlay of a few pounds on a large-scale Ordnance Survey map is money well spent. This will show the geography of the coast in great detail, including the access roads and paths. Intelligent use of the details can often lead to first-class fishing in unfamiliar areas. It is good practice, particularly in rock fishing to thoroughly survey the area to be fished from high ground during the low-tide period. The ground configuration shows up clearly and a map can be made on graph paper. Using points of reference that will not be covered by water when the tide is full, the exact position of gullies, overhangs, deep holes (a good bet for big fish), kelp beds and so on, can all be noted (see page 14).

This helps one to fish objectively and to place a bait where it will do the most good. It also economises on end tackle when bottom fishing. Great care must be exercised when fishing from a rock-bound coast. All too easily, an angler can be attracted to high ground fronting the sea without giving adequate thought to a line of retreat when the tide makes up. This situation often leads to anglers being cut off by the tide with many such incidents ending in tragedy. Shorefishing from rocky stations can be hazardous in areas where there is a sweep of tide. Huge waves arrive on the coast without warning, even though the sea may appear reasonably calm. A wall of water only three feet high has incredible power and will claw its way as much as 30 feet up a cliff face.

Fishing at lonely places should be arranged with a companion, and at best with a small party. It is also good sense to let someone at home know where you are going and the approximate time you expect to return. This is especially important when embarking on a night trip. The need for care at all times cannot be over-emphasised.

Admiralty charts covering a specific area are a great asset to the boat fisherman. In addition to deep water they show principal estuaries, harbours and the larger tidal rivers. The type of bottom and depth of water is clearly marked. All buoys and lights from lighthouses, navigation aids on shore, high ground and prominent land marks are detailed.

There are three distinct categories available to the boat fisherman. Fishing from small craft which can be towed behind the family car, or hired for the day or half-day at many places, is growing rapidly in popularity. The main advantage is mobility, which gives an opportunity to fish new places at a low cost.

Charter boat fishing has become a highly-organised business. Large fleets of fully-licensed craft are based at many ports. Skippers of what are termed 'reef boats' confine their activities to fishing rocky and open ground. In most cases these boats are equal of craft engaged in deep-water wreck fishing, with identical life-saving equipment and fully licensed by a local authority for operations within a prescribed area, the allowable distance from land varying from port to port. The difference between them and wreck fishing, apart from the cost of a day's fishing, which is slightly cheaper, is a Decca Navigator, which locates the wreck without difficulty, providing a skipper has a set of co-ordinate numbers. A few craft have Board of Trade licences as well as a local

Shorefishing Seasonal Chart

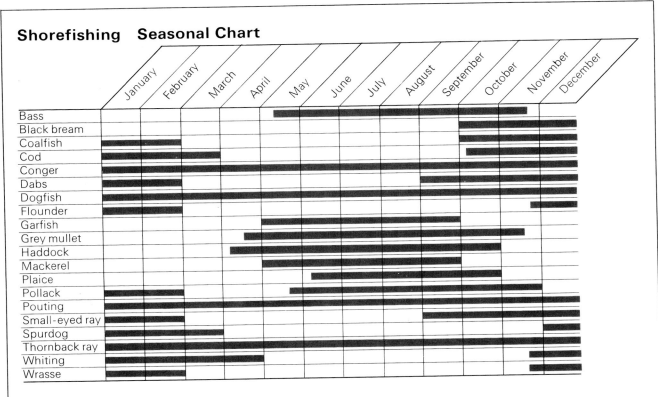

	January	February	March	April	May	June	July	August	September	October	November	December
Bass					████	████	████	████	████	████		
Black bream									████	████	████	████
Coalfish	████	████							████	████	████	
Cod	████										████	████
Conger												
Dabs								████	████	████	████	████
Dogfish	████											
Flounder											████	████
Garfish					████	████	████	████	████			
Grey mullet				████	████	████	████	████	████	████		
Haddock				████	████	████	████					
Mackerel					████	████	████	████	████			
Plaice						████	████	████	████	████	████	████
Pollack	████	████	████	████	████	████	████	████	████	████	████	████
Pouting	████	████	████								████	████
Small-eyed ray								████	████	████	████	████
Spurdog	████	████	████									
Thornback ray	████	████	████	████								
Whiting	████	████	████								████	████
Wrasse	████	████										

Boat Fishing Seasonal Chart

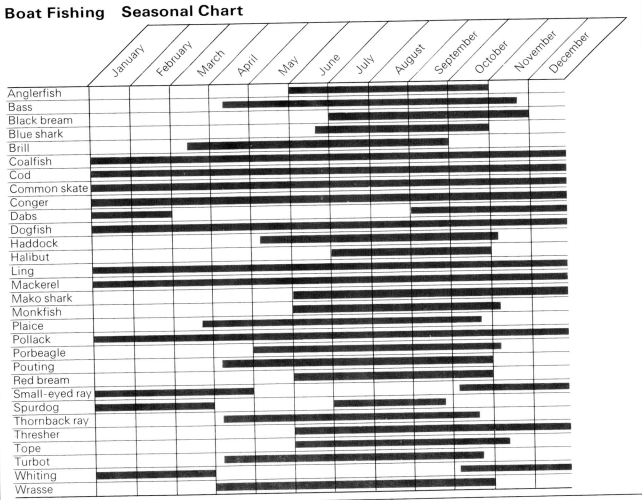

	January	February	March	April	May	June	July	August	September	October	November	December
Anglerfish						████	████	████	████			
Bass					████	████	████	████	████	████		
Black bream						████	████	████	████	████		
Blue shark						████	████	████				
Brill				████	████	████	████	████	████			
Coalfish	████	████	████	████	████	████	████	████	████	████	████	████
Cod	████	████	████	████	████	████	████	████	████	████	████	████
Common skate	████	████	████	████	████	████	████	████	████	████	████	████
Conger	████	████	████						████	████	████	████
Dabs	████	████	████	████								
Dogfish					████	████	████	████	████	████		
Haddock							████	████				
Halibut						████	████	████	████	████		
Ling	████	████	████	████	████	████	████	████	████	████	████	████
Mackerel	████	████	████									
Mako shark						████	████	████	████			
Monkfish					████	████	████	████	████			
Plaice				████	████	████	████	████	████	████		
Pollack												
Porbeagle						████	████	████	████	████		
Pouting						████	████	████	████	████		
Red bream						████	████	████	████	████	████	
Small-eyed ray	████	████	████						████	████		
Spurdog	████	████	████									
Thornback ray				████	████	████	████	████	████	████	████	████
Thresher					████	████	████	████	████	████		
Tope					████	████	████	████	████			
Turbot									████	████	████	████
Whiting	████	████										
Wrasse					████	████	████	████	████	████		

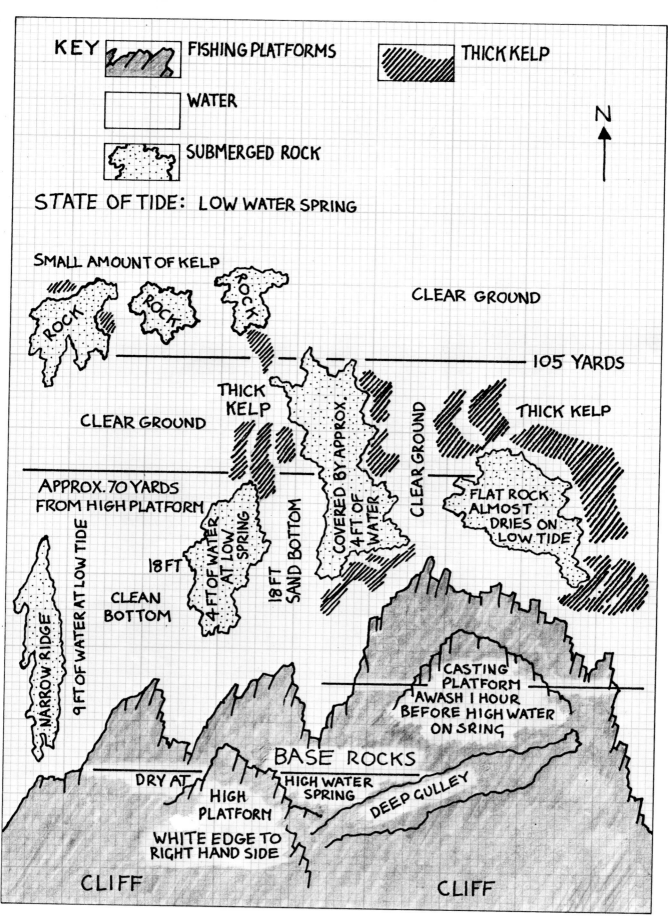

Left In order to fish for large fish it is necessary to first catch the bait. One of the most effective and popular fish baits is mackerel and here three are landed after being caught with the traditional lure: feathers.

Opposite It is good practice to make a record of the main features of an area being fished, especially from rocks, so that if you should return the best fishing places, as well as the hazards, are remembered.

operator certificate which allows him to operate as much as 50 miles from land. Before embarking on either trip a newcomer to boat fishing should pay careful heed to the chapter dealing specifically with the subject, as there are many pitfalls for the uninitiated.

Deep-water reef fishing is available at most places between April and late October but wrecking is usually a year-round affair. The majority of skippers engaging in it are full-time professionals, often operating the craft for an owner. When charter parties are not available he simply switches to some form of commercial fishing as the cost of keeping a boat fitted with a mass of electronic gear at a mooring is astronomical.

The high cost of a day afloat has led to a decline in the number of anglers participating in wreck fishing expeditions. On average, the fee for a top-class boat is about £10 a head, if a full complement of ten anglers is aboard. A smaller number will push up the cost considerably as the missing rods have to be compensated by those who are aboard. It is always wise to find out just what you are letting yourself in for before leaving the quay.

There is a classic story of the visitor to a certain West Country port who, to his delight, obtained at very short notice a place on a charter boat. He was even more pleased when he found only three others aboard on what was obviously going to be a day of perfect weather. On returning to port with a fine catch of fish, he was shocked when settling his bill. By simply not enquiring about the cost before setting off his wallet was £25 lighter. Unwittingly, he had become a member of a privately-chartered boat as opposed to going on a fishing trip as an individual. Salt was rubbed into the wound when he also found he was allowed to take only two fish away. It is almost a cardinal rule that expensive charter boats do not sail with just four anglers aboard paying £10 a head.

A thorough working knowledge of the tides and how they affect the movement of fish is vital. A set of tide tables is essential if a fishing trip is to be planned with precision. Most tackle shops sell a small booklet giving tidal movements throughout the year. A valuable aid is a tidal atlas showing the run and strength of water during a complete tide over a given stretch of coast.

Spring tides, when the greatest movement of water is experienced, occur at the new and full moon. Neaps, which are the smallest tides, occur at the moon's quarters. High water varies from one day to the next by as little as half an hour during spring tides, but more than $1\frac{1}{2}$ hours during neaps. The flow of water during the normal length tide is $6\frac{1}{4}$ hours and works out at roughly one-twelfth of the total in each of the first and final hours, two-twelfths in the second and fourth hours, and three-twelfths in the third and fifth hours.

The effect of wind on tidal streams should never be underestimated. Wind blowing against the tide in the shallows can raise quite a chop. Where the water is deeper the surface currents of the tidal stream decrease as an opposing wind increases in force but a wind blowing with the tide strengthens the drift.

It is commonsense to obtain a detailed weather forecast before setting off on a fishing trip, particularly if going afloat. The information should be obtained from the meteorological office nearest to the area being fished. Stations are positioned all around the coastline of the British Isles and the officer on duty will give precise details on the general conditions, visibility, wind speed and direction, and the outlook for 12 hours ahead. The 'Met' office forecast should not be confused with the Post Office variety, which is simply a recorded message giving weather of a general nature.

It is often said that sports fishing has four stages. The beginner's ambition is to catch something, irrespective of size or species. Once this has been achieved the second stage is to catch a lot and return home after each trip laden with fish. This brings an accolade from neighbours and enables the angler to bask in the glow of success while friends feast on the fish bounteously bestowed. This leads directly to the specimen hunting stage, in which only the very largest of fish is of interest. Some anglers then develop a passion for landing these on ultra-light tackle or, to perform what seems the impossible.

All this takes some years and it is only then that a sea angler begins to appreciate the full joy of fishing, which comes with the realisation that the making of any kind of catch is secondary to being involved in Britain's most popular pastime.

Basic shorefishing tackle and rigs

Rods

Experienced anglers choose rods to match their sport. On the East Coast of England, where successful cod fishing is tied to long-range casting, very powerful tournament-style rods are popular. As they are used in rod rests weight is unimportant and even the most powerful rods are sensitive enough to detect cod bites, which are typically vicious. The cod angler is therefore prepared to sacrifice a measure of finesse to gain those extra 20 yards range.

Bass anglers working the rocks and surf beaches of Cornwall face different conditions. Although distance is important, the rod action must be smooth and pliable to allow easy casting from difficult terrain where full pendulum techniques are impossible to perform. Bass can be wild biters but they are more likely to nibble the bait. Tournament rods are too dull to pick out those minute trembles on the line which signal a surf bass. Overall, then, the design emphasis is on lightness, sensitivity and modest casting power.

Despite the complexity of our shore fishing, it is possible to buy a set of tackle that handles almost any branch of the sport, will cast extremely well and, most important, will offer a beginner the very best opportunity to learn to cast those 100 yards-plus distances so necessary for success.

Look for a good glass fibre rod, between 11 and 12 ft long. The rod should attain peak performance with a 5 oz sinker which is the weight best suited to long-range casting and to the majority of shore fishing conditions. Be wary of straying outside that length recommendation because a rod too long or too short kills any chance of casting well. There is a lot of argument about preferred rod length but experienced anglers confirm that for all forward-facing casts (see casting techniques chapter) the $11\frac{1}{2}$ ft rod holds its own in any company. However, in the early days, 6 inches either way has little effect.

The need for a glass fibre rod is stressed not because carbon is inferior — it is actually a far better rod material — but because good carbon rods are expensive. There is no point in buying one until you are deeply committed to the sport and until you understand exactly which type of length, power and action suit you best. An excellent glass rod may cost less than £50. Good carbon beachcasters are still £100 or more, hence the wisdom of knowing requirements before handing over cash.

Some rods are built in two equal sections joined by a spigot; others have a long tip (about $8\frac{1}{2}$ ft long) coupled to a short butt. Both constructions are excellent but long-tip rods are usually more specialised in design and application. They are also more difficult to transport and easier to break by accident.

There is no better way to choose a rod than to test it beforehand, preferably in company with a competent caster who can demonstrate the rod's capabilities. More insight will be gained into rod design in half-an-hour this way than in 20 years of trial and error. However, there are some clear pointers to good design and, with care, you can avoid major pitfalls even if personal help cannot be found.

Never buy a rod with a 'sloppy' butt section. Stiffness in the butt is essential for good casting and fishing. Thus, immediately eliminate from the list any rod described as 'reverse taper', 'butt action' and 'through action'. An easy test is to place the butt cap against the floor, support the rod at the spigot joint, then push down on the centre of the butt section. Around 50 lb of pressure should flex the butt 3 inches.

A tackle dealer demonstrates a 12 lb class rod's test curve to a customer. To a knowledgeable angler the shape of the rod curve is far more important than fancy fittings or an illustrious name.

Rods too floppy to pass this test can be discounted. Extremely stiff rods, though excellent for casting, must be viewed with suspicion at this stage because their butt rigidity is usually accompanied by a very fast, unforgiving casting action which exaggerates error.

The top three feet of the rod must be pliable enough for good casting and sensitive bite indication. Most rods are satisfactory; it is rare to discover a modern shorecasting rod with a tip too stiff for adequate response.

The middle section of the rod, though critically important for the advanced angler, is of little concern to the beginner.

It should form a smooth, logical progression of thickness and stiffness between the tip and the butt. This is indicative of a medium-fast action which is perfect for general beach fishing.

Most rods have rubber handle grips of either a single sheath from butt cap to reel seat or in three separate handgrips. Some cheap rods, and a very few high-class beachcasters, still retain cork grips which are warm and comfortable to hold. However, the material is generally obsolescent in modern sea fishing.

There can be no compromise on the position and security of the reel seat. If it is too high or too low, you can never learn to

The right tackle in the right place at the right time; two fine bass caught with a light bass rod from an Atlantic storm beach.

cast long distances. As a guide, if the reel sits between 27 and 32 inches away from the butt cap, the rod is fine. Outside that, expect inefficiency and poor handling.

Conventional screw winch fittings in stainless steel, carbon/nylon and high impact plastics are a good choice, as are Fuji clips and even simple hoseclips. Insist on a fitting that holds the reel securely in the right place. Nothing else really matters at this stage.

The vast majority of production rods are correctly ringed with hard-chrome wire or aluminium oxide lined guides. If possible, pick a rod with aluminium oxide linings because they are stronger and smoother

than wire, which usually distort and corrode in time.

The tip ring ought to be stainless steel if the internal diameter of the ring exceeds 16 mm. Above that, aluminium oxide linings are unreliable because the leader knot can tear the guide from its cushion ring. But avoid tungsten carbide tips. They are far too brittle for use on a beach. You can fish with a broken side ring, but a smashed tip brings casting to a halt.

A beginner need not be concerned with ring spacings and sizes. Around seven side rings, from 12 mm at the tip to 25 or 30 mm at the butt, serve well for both fixed-spool and multiplier reel casting.

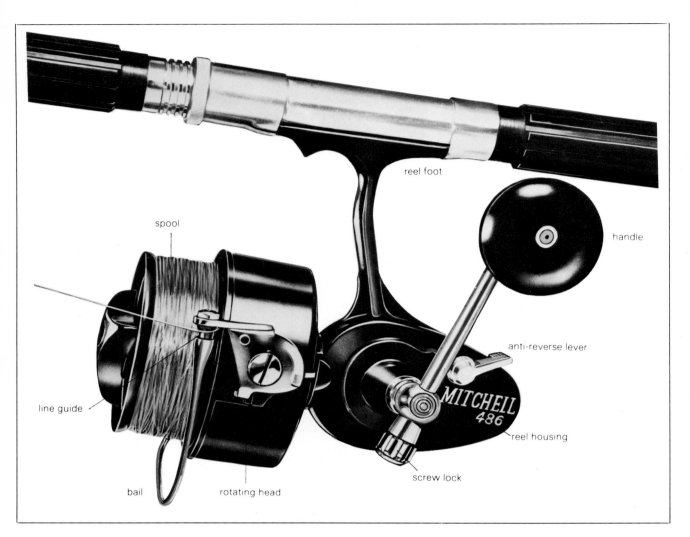

reel foot

spool

handle

line guide

anti-reverse lever

MITCHELL 486

reel housing

screw lock

bail

rotating head

Standard fixed-spool reel: the Mitchell 486.

Theoretically, each reel should have a complementary ringing pattern. In practice, production rods work well with either reel unless you can cast very well indeed. Avoid the special fixed-spool rods if you plan to use a multiplier. You can get away with using a fixed-spool on a multiplier-ringed rod but you will have headaches using a multiplier on a rod with only three giant rings.

Shorecasting reels

Only fixed-spool and multiplier reels are of interest to the dedicated beach angler. Side-cast reels and centre-pins may be regarded as obsolete, for they neither cast far enough nor match today's rods.

Fixed-spool reels allow line to peel off from the forward lip of the spool, the axis of which points towards the rod rings. Multipliers feed line from a rotating spool. Both systems cast extremely well and handle most kinds of fishing but the multiplier has the edge in balance, smoothness and all-

round precision. It is the first choice of the angler who wants to get the very best from his sport. On the other hand, the multiplier will not tolerate bad casting techniques. It is a nightmare for an unskilled beginner.

The fixed-spool is very easy to use and can be mastered in an hour. The obvious recommendation is that a self-taught novice will benefit from the fixed-spool reel, mainly because he will, at least, get his baits into the water most of the time. But if he is coached in basic techniques of casting, it does not matter which reel he chooses because it is technique that determines whether or not the multiplier overruns every cast. In fact, a multiplier is no more difficult to operate than a fixed-spool if you look at it this way. Ideally, every angler should use both reels, for there are times when each is superior.

The fixed-spool equals the multiplier for distance casting. The differences between the reels are largely subjective. It so happens that most anglers prefer to fish with a multiplier for personal reasons. In purely objective terms, the fixed-spool probably has the advantage of speed, reliability, versatility and perhaps in ultimate casting range as well.

Suitable multiplier reels for beach fishing include the ABU Ambassadeur 6500C, 7000, 8000C and 9000C; Penn 100, 146, 140, 150; Newell 220F, 229F, 323F; and the Mitchell 600 series. Essential features are lightweight spools, precision bearings, strong frames and robust gears.

Check the specifications of the listed reels and you find there are two sizes of multipliers available: small and medium reels holding 200-275 yards of 15 lb nylon; larger reels extend the capacity to over 400 yards. Where possible, use the smallest reel compatible with your kind of fishing. The small reels generally cast farther and more easily and are more for-giving of errors. But there are occasions when you will need a big reel with great reserves of line, or which accommodates sufficient heavy nylon in the 30-45 lb class.

The fixed-spool market includes the Mitchell 498 and 486, the DAM Quick 5000 and the Sagarra Tarzan. High capacity reels are preferred because they cast farther. Cast 150 yards from a small reel and the line level is so reduced that casting effort is absorbed by line friction on the rim of the spool. On a very large reel, the line level stays up near the rim, which might add 25 yards to the cast. The snag is that big reels are heavy and cumbersome, but in this case you cannot have it both ways; either cast well and suffer restrictions on the tackle balance or use a lightweight reel and watch the bait drop short of the fish.

Apart from spool dimension, the most

Typical of the beach casting multiplier reels is the Mitchell 600 series.

crush-proof fibreglass spool

free-spool lever

reel foot

star wheel

handle

21

important design feature of a fixed-spool reel is a powerful clutch that locks the spool solid for casting. If the spool slips in mid-cast, the line cuts your finger to the bone.

Another problem on some reels is that the bale arm closes in mid-cast, bringing proceedings to an abrupt halt. Many reels now incorporate anti-inertia devices to prevent early closure. Top casters cut off the bale arm wire as a matter of routine. Two reels, the Mitchell 498 and the Sagarra Tarzan have simple manual roller pick-ups which do not need to swing back for casting. This is the perfect answer.

All the reels named here are chosen because they are well tried and popular. Each is built to high engineering standards from first-rate materials with gears that are strong and smooth and brake systems that are powerful and sensitive. Frames and reel seats resist the pressures of hard casting and servicing and spare parts are readily available.

When it comes to sophistication, you get what you pay for. The higher-priced multi-pliers have centrifugal brakes (not an essential feature), ballrace bearings and high speed gearings. Even the cheapest reels on the list can cast to extreme range and will beat any fish likely to be hooked in British waters.

Lines

Nylon monofilament is the only line for beach fishing. Braided materials like Dacron have no place because they neither cast nor handle well enough for distance work. Their only remote application might be in specialised conger eel and skate fishing from rocks.

Nylon is tough, cheap and reliable with good brands that cast well, form excellent knots and withstand every fishing pressure. What is more, the reel line does not require vast breaking strain. On open ground, 15 lb nylon is more than adequate; sometimes 10 lb line is tough enough. There is still a strong case to be made for heavier lines on rocky beaches where tackle and fish are manhandled through weeds and obstructions. A line of 25 to 50 lb is a realistic choice but higher breaking strains are physically impossible to exploit because a fishing rod is such an inefficient lever.

The chief considerations, apart from reliability and general quality, are even diameter and softness. You cannot cast your best with a wiry monofilament, not even with a fixed-spool reel. The more inert the line, the better it is. In turn, the easier you can cast, the more confident you are and the farther out to sea the bait falls.

Expensive lines are not necessarily better or even the best choice. There are good casting and fishing lines like Milbro, Triple Fish, Sylcast and DAM Strike that may cost as little as £2.50 for over 1000 yards of 15 lb breaking strain on a bulk spool. They are highly recommended for practice casting and general fishing.

However, more expensive lines offer higher breaking strain for less diameter and many of them are tougher on the surface, which shrugs off abrasion from sand and stones. If you drop the line breaking strain below, say, 12 lb test, consider Maxima, Stren, Berkley and Platil. They cost up to 20 times as much as the cheaper lines but the expense is justified for specialised beach fishing. They are definitely not intended for a beginner who over-runs a multiplier too often.

Nylon of 15 lb is the first choice because it casts very well and is strong enough. On most small/medium reels, it provides a useful capacity of at least 220 yards which is plenty, except for tope fishing where the fish strips off a lot of line on its initial run out to sea. Generally, steer clear of thick lines because so much range is lost and more lead is needed to anchor the tackle against the tide.

Hooks

At fishing ranges over 75 yards it is impossible to strike the hook into a fish's jaw. You rely on needle-sharp hooks, efficient traces and the co-operation of the fish itself. As the hook is the obvious weak link in the system, you must ensure its design and presentation are first-rate. There can be no compromise here. Probably more fish are lost through poor hooking than for any other reason.

Great strength in the hook is not necessary for most species of fish. Fine wire hooks are better all round as they cause less trauma to the bait, present it more neatly and are far sharper. Aberdeen hooks from Mustad and Cannelle (Au Lion d'Or) are widely available. Partridge, the British hookmaker, produce high quality hooks, among them the Breakaway Spearspade. For tough species such as conger eels,

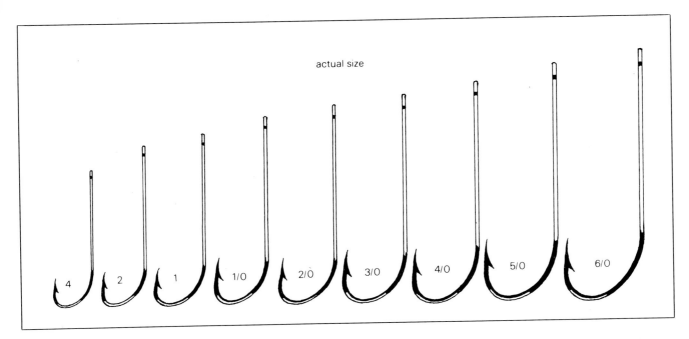

actual size

4   2   1   1/0   2/0   3/0   4/0   5/0   6/0

A typical range of hooks shown actual size.

rays and tope, O'Shaughnessy and Viking patterns offer greater strength in the shank. Strongest of all is the Mustad Seamaster, a specialised game-fishing hook.

Hooks are available with eyes or spade ends. Both are good but spade ends must be tied carefully or they will tear from the trace under pressure. Everything taken into consideration, the eyed hook is better but just make sure the eyes are small and neat.

Hook size specifications are a mess. The traditional numbering systems are unnecessarily complex and inconsistent between manufacturers. A better guide is to ignore the number on the box and measure the gape, which is the length of a perpendicular line from shank to point.

Basically, small hooks and big hooks are needed. For winter cod, big whiting, rays, tope and bass, choose a hook with a 15-20 mm gape. The bigger the bait, the bigger the hook should be, so include that factor in the equation.

Small fish, including flatfish, eels and anything under about 4 lb require a gape between 5 and 15 mm. These two size ranges correspond to hook sizes commonly referred to as 1/0, 6/0 and 4-1/0. However, one maker's size 1/0 might equal 3/0 elsewhere. Measure the gape yourself and you will soon select hooks automatically.

Weights

Smooth casting, power to hold the seabed and sufficient momentum to carry the baits through the air are the essential functions of a lead weight for sea fishing. From experience in fishing and tournament casting, approximately 5 oz of lead are perfect for all but the most delicate angling or for blasting a bait into gales. When familiar with casting, you may discover that even $\frac{1}{2}$ oz variations make a lot of difference to the fishing distances achieved.

If wind and weather are against you, do not hesitate to use 6 or even 8 oz of lead. You will not hit peak casting range but at least your baits will stay out in the sea instead of being swept ashore in the breakers. At the other extreme, just 1 oz of lead is sufficient to cast a small bait 30 yards from the rocks into deep water. But most of the time a 5 oz weight is best.

All good casting weights conform to a torpedo or bomb shape. Advanced ballistics are not involved in beach casting. A sinker is needed which does not flit or tumble in flight, that is all. In addition, a bomb design is the best compromise between good casting and adequate anchorage on the seabed.

Gripping power is greatly increased by the addition of springy wires to the nose or flanks of the sinker. Permanent wires provide most grip, though quite hard to retrieve through rough ground.

An alternative weight design has swivelling wires, held in position by sprung beads or elastic bands. When line tension (at the beginning of the retrieve) overcomes the wires' grip to the seabed they flip backwards to trail behind the weight, eliminating the drag. The sinker is available

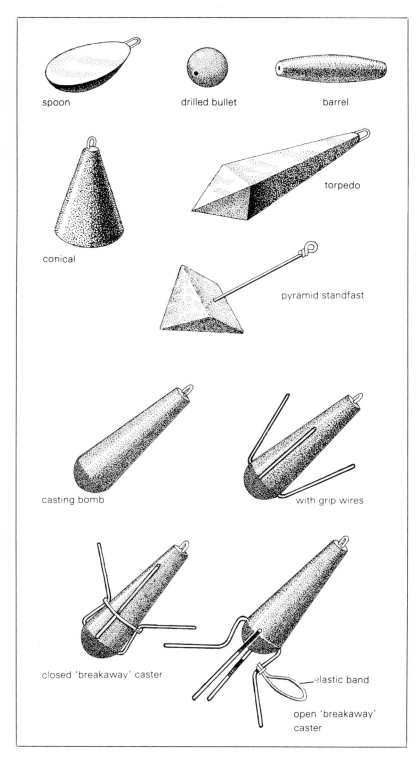

spoon

drilled bullet

barrel

conical

torpedo

pyramid standfast

casting bomb

with grip wires

closed 'breakaway' caster

elastic band

open 'breakaway' caster

with a swivel moulded into the tail. When new, they are strong enough but once the brass has corroded and strained the swivel can rip apart.

Tackle assembly

Filling the multiplier reel with line. Tie the end of the line to the spool core. A timber hitch is the standard knot because it is strong and neat. Now wind on the line as neatly as possible, laying the coils smoothly back and forth across the whole width of the reel. The level-wind mechanism on some reels does this automatically but finger and thumb are better. Be sure to maintain tension on the line because loose coils of nylon are a menace. There is no need to partly fill the spool with soft backing, which used to be specified on older reels. If there is room for backing the reel is too big, anyway. If backing is needed to prevent the nylon smashing the reel, you bought the wrong reel. Modern spools are strong enough to resist all normal fishing pressures.

Fill the spool almost full but do not cram on every possible last yard. A line level around $\frac{3}{16}$ inch down from the rim is better for casting because it reduces the tendency to over-run.

Filling the fixed-spool reel with line. Fill the spool right up to the rim with 15 lb nylon, wound on nice and tight. Because most of the recommended casting reels hold so much line, back the main line with old monofilament or waterproof string. The amount of backing should be gauged by trial and error; aim to use about 250 yards of main line on top. On big spools this means filling with backing to within about $\frac{1}{2}$ inch of the rim. If unsure of the correct level for filling, wind on some extra line. Many top casters deliberately overload the fixed-spool in order to reduce rim friction to the minimum.

Tying on the shock leader. 15 lb line cannot withstand the shock of casting so buffer the line by inserting a length of heavy monofilament between reel and sinker. This is called a shock leader and is normally of 35-50 lb breaking strain; 40 lb is ideal for learning to cast. Make sure the nylon is really soft and inert.

Attach the reel to the rod, then thread the leader DOWN the rings from tip to butt. Tie the leader neatly to the reel line with the

A selection of popular lead weights and sinkers used in shorefishing and casting.

Opposite bottom Every angler needs to know a few simple knots. Here are some of the more basic knots for tying on hooks, swivels or joining lengths of line.

commercially as the Breakaway but anglers can make their own from modified aluminium moulds.

From the safety angle, it is essential that the tail loop is strong and well buried in the lead. Brass, or better still, stainless steel wire are good. Never use plain steel because it rusts away and then snaps under load. It is as well to avoid bombs

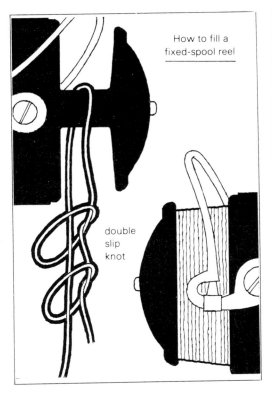

How to fill a fixed-spool reel

double slip knot

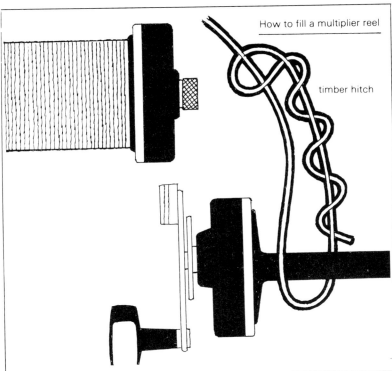

How to fill a multiplier reel

timber hitch

illustrated knot. Now rotate the reel handle until six turns of leader are on the spool. This is the minimum number of coils for safety.

Measure down from the rod tip to the butt ring or even to the reel and cut off the far end of the leader at that point. This provides a strong shock piece which will shrug off a full power cast and is long enough to help haul a big fish through the surf.

Check the leader with every cast and replace it when necessary. It will be seen that when ready to cast a fresh leader, the reel holds more than the six turns specified. This is extra insurance and also means the trace end can be trimmed back several times before the leader becomes too short.

Assembling the basic paternoster rig. Materials and accessories required: strong oval split ring 10 mm long; strong plain swivel at least 15 mm long; 4 ft nylon leader; 4 inch narrow bore plastic tubing (an old Biro refill tube); trace and hook (for cod fishing, 20-25 lb nylon and 15 mm gape fine wire hook).

Tie the swivel to one end of the leader

Above right How to fill a multiplier reel with line. Tie the nylon securely to the spool core, using the spool slot where provided, with a timber hitch knot. Fill the spool evenly so that the coils lie flat (like on a cotton reel); do not overload.
Above left How to fill a fixed-spool reel with line. Secure the nylon to the spool core with a simple double slip knot and wind on line under firm pressure to the edge of the rim.

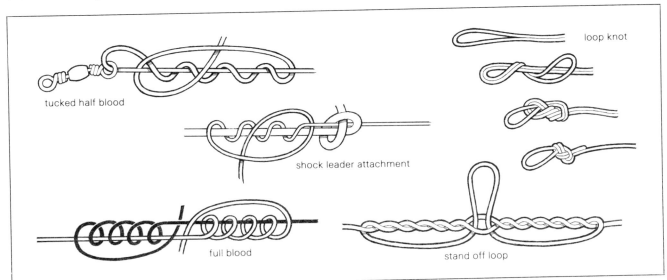

tucked half blood

loop knot

shock leader attachment

full blood

stand off loop

material using a tucked half-blood knot. Attach the split ring to the other end with the same knot.

Measure down 18 inches from the swivel, form a loop 6 inches across and tie in a stand-off loop. Make sure the coils of nylon snuggle down against each other and tighten evenly. Slide the tubing over the loop to stiffen it. Make up the hook snood; tie the hook to the trace nylon with a tucked half-blood knot; cut off the trace to length and tie a loop at the end. Fix the snood to the stand-off loop by interlocking the loops, reef-knot style.

Tie the swivel to the shock leader with the tucked half-blood knot and clip the tail loop of the sinker to the split ring. The trace is now ready to bait and cast but do not forget to sharpen the hook first.

Other terminal rigs. The one-hook paternoster in its most basic form is the best all-rounder for beach fishing. It casts well, attracts fish and drives home the hook effectively. It is also cheap and reliable. Little wonder, then, that many beach

A selection of the most popular and widely-used rigs in shorefishing, including the basic paternoster and running leger rigs.

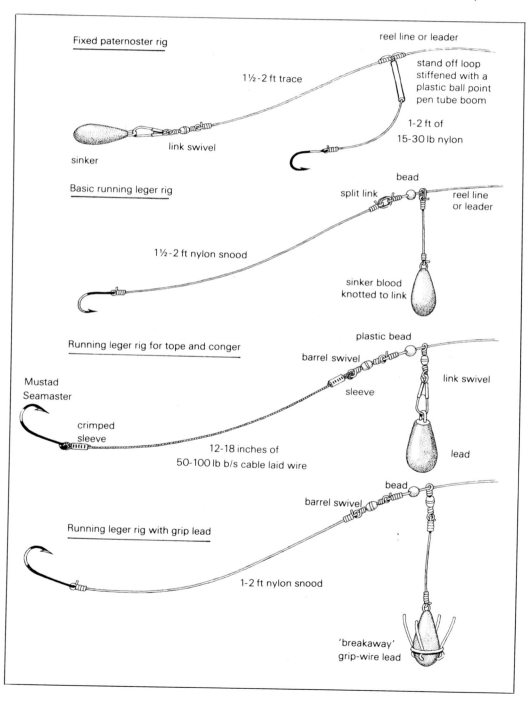

Fixed paternoster rig

reel line or leader

stand off loop stiffened with a plastic ball point pen tube boom

1½-2 ft trace

1-2 ft of 15-30 lb nylon

link swivel

sinker

Basic running leger rig

bead

split link

reel line or leader

1½-2 ft nylon snood

sinker blood knotted to link

Running leger rig for tope and conger

plastic bead

barrel swivel

link swivel

Mustad Seamaster

sleeve

crimped sleeve

12-18 inches of 50-100 lb b/s cable laid wire

lead

bead

barrel swivel

Running leger rig with grip lead

1-2 ft nylon snood

'breakaway' grip-wire lead

fishermen never use anything else.

The paternoster can be modified to take two or three hooks. Just tie in as many stand-off loops as you need, then add the snoods cut short so they do not intertwine. There is some argument on trace length. Some anglers say light, long snoods are best; others swear by a short, stiff hook section. A lot depends on where you fish, so be ready to follow local tradition which is usually based on sound principles.

If possible, use short, fairly stiff snoods because they fly better and help the bait stay on the hook. The less air drag and more strength built into the paternoster the farther will be the cast and the easier it will be to land a good fish. Stiffer traces do not tangle so readily which is an important point with fixed-spool work.

Other rigs include running legers and a cross-breed of paternoster and leger. All have their devotees and, indeed, it pays to be flexible in approach. Learn from local experience but if in doubt stick to the paternoster.

The broad theme of trace design is the

The simplest and most common shorefishing rig — the paternoster — being used with a gripwire sinker and ragworm bait. This type of tackle is cheap and easy to produce, casts extremely well and places baits right down on the seabed.

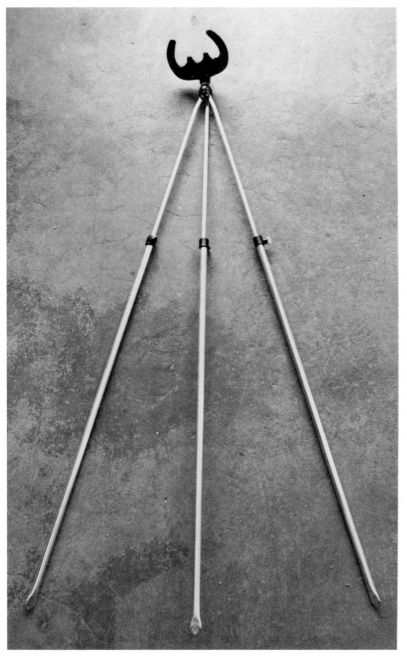

An essential part of the shore angler's equipment is a rod rest. Illustrated are the monopod (*right*) and the tripod (*left*).

elimination of everything that does not serve a useful purpose. Too many swivels, wire booms and other gadgets only increase weight and reduce the cast. Most add little or nothing to the efficiency of the rig. Swivels, for example, hardly ever rotate which makes them an expensive alternative to a split ring. Beaded paternosters are an exception to the rule; the extra work involved helps overcome trace tangling.

Booms are not obsolete, despite what some of the experts claim. Some years ago, when distance casting was new to British shore angling, traces were cut to the bone, often to their detriment. Most good anglers now use lightweight, aerodynamically sound booms made from plastic or stainless steel. Avoid the old-fashioned Christmas trees of brass and scrap iron. Kilmore and Clements booms are useless as well.

Beach fishing accessories

Rod rests. A good rod rest is worth its weight in gold. Avoid flimsy tripods which tip over when the rod is leaned against them. Better invest in a heavy beach spike or conventional stake with a rod holder at the top. Bash them into the sand and shingle and they will not fold up under the pressures of tackle and tide. The more robust tripods are reasonably good for fishing from concrete walls and jetties but inferior to the old types of rests. Rigidity and strength are essential. A rod holder lined with rubber is also needed to prevent the rod being slashed to ribbons.

Lanterns for night fishing. Night fishing offers the best sport, so you must be geared up to spend hours out there in the dark. A high-power paraffin lamp is essential. Torches and the smaller gas lamps are useless as a main light. Get the most powerful lamp obtainable. Better still, buy two. Electric lamps are useful for spotlighting the rod tip and for baiting up because they inject brilliant light on to the scene. They supplement the main light but never depend on them.

Thumb and finger stalls. Long-distance casting is hard on fingers and thumbs. Even a modest cast will tear the skin if the line slips. Leather finger and thumb stalls are standard equipment for hard casting but adhesive plaster strips or the finger cut from an old rubber glove can be used. Full finger protection is necessary for fixed-spool work. For multiplier casting use a ring of rubber cut from an old household glove. This leaves the tip of the thumb nice and sensitive for reel control but still protects the soft skin which initially holds down the spool. Confidence gained with finger or thumb protection may well add 25 yards to the cast.

Bait knife and pliers. Buy a high-quality knife which takes and keeps a razor edge. It pays for itself time after time for gutting, filleting the catch and for cutting baits. Cheap knives are not worth buying. Pliers help to make good traces and their side cutters trim nylon and wire. Long-nose pliers are better than conventional disgorgers. Keep the pliers lightly oiled to resist salt spray corrosion.

Tackle bags and boxes. Carrier seats are ideal for storing masses of tackle and to sit on when fishing. They are too heavy and bulky for rock fishing or for trailing miles along the sands when light haversacks and rucksacks are better. Bits and pieces of tackle are best stored in plastic boxes with tightly-fitting lids. Transparent lids allow a view of what is inside the box without opening the contents to wind and rain.

Clothing. Buy the finest clothing obtainable. One-piece suits are good but separate jacket and trousers are handy because you are not committed to dressing up when you do not need to. Choose between an unlined waterproof plus a thermal undersuit, or buy an outfit with fixed insulation. The choice depends on where and when you mostly fish. Wellingtons and thigh waders are standard footwear. Chest-high waders are specialised equipment for surfcasting on storm beaches. They are too bulky and uncomfortable for general use. Insulated 'moon boots' are superior footwear for winter beach fishing.

When night fishing some form of artificial light is needed to illuminate the rod tip; the most popular is the paraffin pressure lantern like this Tilley lamp.

Natural baits

King rag is undoubtedly one of the boat angler's favourite baits, especially over reefs and wrecks where over the years it has been responsible for a stream of specimen fish.

The objective which all anglers strive for is to present the right bait in the right place at the right time but this is seldom achieved with any degree of consistency. It is a measure of an angler's skill when he can accurately assess where and when the fish will be feeding and on which type of bait. A very important factor is pre-planning and research and could well be called an expert's secret weapon. Research is often troublesome and time-consuming but it

forms the basis of objective experience which will pay dividends for the whole of an angling career, multiplying chances of success by at least the factor of two.

The right bait is another essential factor. It often proves a real difficulty for inland anglers who do not have the benefit of on the spot local knowledge to find out what bait the fish are feeding on at a given moment. Friendly contact with a local angler, sea angling club, bait or tackle

dealer can often put you on the right track, perhaps obtaining or reserving bait on your behalf.

Buying bait is an expensive but often unavoidable way to obtain the best baits. The ideal situation would be to have sufficient time to devote to gathering baits from the area adjacent to where one intends to fish. Bait dug locally will almost always outfish bait imported from another area.

The correct choice of bait depends on species and season, but research and planning will ensure that as far as possible one arrives in the right place with the correct tackle and complete with the right bait.

Fresh natural baits can be found all along our coastline, in harbours, creeks, beaches and rockpools. It depends largely on the species of fish you seek where you go to locate the bait suited to each of those species.

Worm baits

These are easily the most popular baits for the shore angler and, to a slightly lesser extent, for the boat angler.

Ragworm. There are three species of ragworm commonly used as bait, king ragworm, the harbour or red and the white. With a little hard work these can be collected from mud creeks and harbours, taking care not to dig out boat moorings and even greater care to avoid areas of deep soft mud, into which you could very easily sink.

Ragworms, usually king rag, are often available for purchase from bait and tackle dealers but advance ordering is often essential as they soon sell out.

King rag is undoubtedly the boat angler's favourite with deadly appeal when used over reefs and, to a lesser extent, the wrecks. Over the years this bait has been responsible for many specimens.

Digging for ragworm is messy and strenuous as they usually live in the heavy black mud of an estuary just above the low tide mark.

King rag is usually found at the extremes of the low tide mark in heavy, black gravelly mud. The average size is 7-8 inches, but in relatively quiet areas of digging activity, where the worm has a chance to grow undisturbed, they can reach lengths of up to 18 inches. All ragworms have a pair of small nippers growing from its head and the king rag is capable of a surprisingly sharp nip; so be warned!

All three types of ragworm are relatively soft in the body so extract them from the mud with great care to avoid breaking them. Broken worms should be separated from whole worms or they will quickly cause the rest of the worms to die. Use broken worms first. When keeping rag monitor them constantly, removing dead or ailing worms immediately.

Ragworm can be kept for a few days in a large cool bait box with some damp seaweed. Commercial worm dealers store their worms in a cool spot in Vermiculite, which also works very well. Ragworm can be kept for several weeks in a sea water aquarium provided the water stays clean and aerated at a cool, constant temperature.

King rag is often used whole when boatfishing, threaded on to a fine wire long-shanked hook so that the tail is left free to move enticingly in undersea currents. Shore anglers tend to use these big worms in smaller pieces, making sure the worm does not slide down the hook shank to collect in a ball in the bend of the hook to mask the hookpoint.

Harbour or red ragworm are identical but smaller replicas of king rag. They are found in the soft mud of creeks and harbours and can be dug quite easily with a small garden fork. The precautions needed to keep king rag apply equally to harbour rag. More often used by shore anglers for float fishing and light legering, harbour rag is sometimes used two or more at a time on a fine wire hook.

White rag are more usually found in clean sand at the extremity of the low tide mark. This is a hardier worm than harbour rag and seems to keep much better in a cool, damp bait box and for longer periods in a saltwater aquarium with clean, cool aerated seawater as the essential factor. White rag is excellent bait for float fishing and when legered has accounted for some surprisingly large specimens. It is a great favourite with competition anglers who often go to great lengths to ensure a supply.

Lugworms are found all round the coastline and much used in those areas which feature cod in the winter months. They are freely available at those places from bait dealers and tackle shops.

There are two types of lugworm, red and black. The red is a deep reddish brown colour, smaller and softer-fleshed than the black variety.

Black lugworms are bigger and often

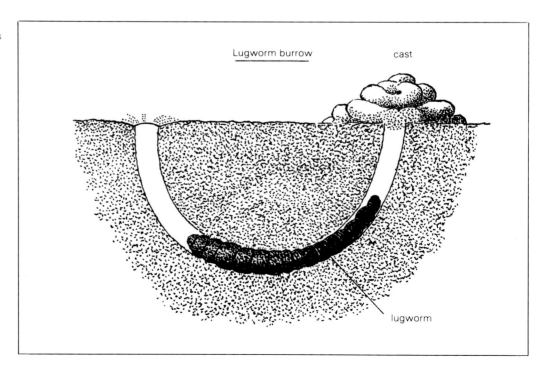

Lugworm burrow   cast

lugworm

better baits than the red but are more difficult to obtain as they are usually much deeper in the sand and spread over a wider area.

Lugworms live in a 'U-shaped' burrow one end of which is indicated by small 'coils' of sand expelled by the worm as it burrows downward. Digging between the two entrances to a lugworm's burrow, below the halfway mark of the receding tide, will soon result in a supply of fresh bait. Any worms damaged in digging should be kept separate from whole worms or they will quickly affect the whole worms. Keep the good worms for a few days in a cool spot, individually wrapped in newspaper. They can be kept alive for much longer periods in an aerated salt-water aquarium.

If keeping lugworms in a deep freeze it is best to use black lug, gutting them by nipping the head and then gently squeezing the body through finger and thumb. Wrap and freeze each worm individually making it easy to take just as many as necessary for each fishing trip.

A single lugworm, threaded on to a longshank hook so that the point emerges halfway down the worm's tail, will suffice for most species of fish. When a larger bait is required two or more worms can be threaded up the line above the hook, so that a tempting bunch of lug is presented to the fish without masking the hook point.

Fish baits

Sandeels are among a sea angler's best baits but, unfortunately, their distribution is limited to the South West coasts of Britain and Eire. They are best used live on light tackle but sandeel fillets and frozen eels are attractive to a lot of species and to flatfishes in particular.

There are two species of sandeel, the lesser sandeel which grows to 6-7 inches and the greater sandeel which grows to at least twice that size. The lesser variety is most used for bait. Supplies are usually obtained from netsmen who surround the shoals with a fine-meshed net and then sell the live eels at a reasonable price. The rest are then often blast-frozen and sold in packets by bait and tackle dealers.

The sandeel's party trick is its ability to burrow into damp sand in the blink of an eye. This is its main line of defence against predators. Buried eels can often be found at the low water extremity of sandy

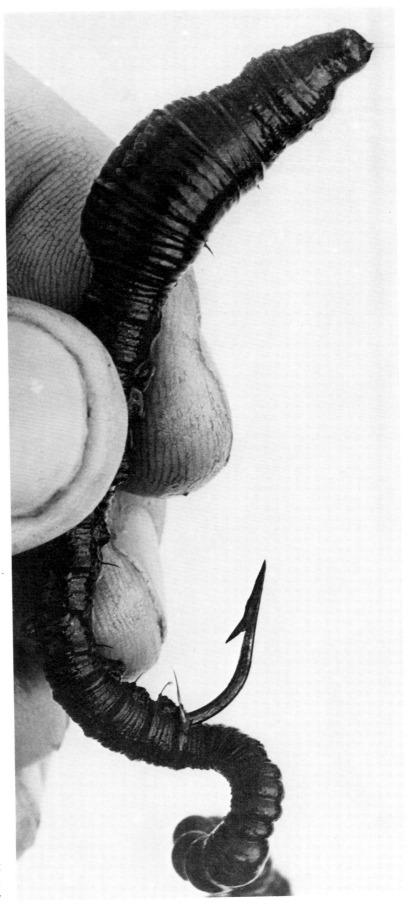

A black and red lugworm.

Opposite top The best way to keep sandeels alive for bait is in a large plastic bucket using a mains or battery-operated aerator. If the seawater is kept cool, clean and well aerated sandeels can be kept for months.

Opposite bottom Two methods of mounting live sandeel as bait.

Opposite Feathering for mackerel; this is the most efficient and simple way of catching this widely-used bait.

beaches and can be dug by the use of a thin-bladed sandeel hook which is cut through the sand until the resistance from the eel's body is felt. A heavily-gloved catching hand is then slid down the blade, trapping the eel against the bend of the hook. The heavy glove is necessary because, infrequently, the resistance felt is from a venomous weaver fish.

Sandeels can be kept alive for a few hours in a cool bait box containing wet sacking or seaweed. They can also be kept in a traditional wicker 'courge', or a perforated wooden box which is allowed to float alongside the boat. But the best method is to use a large plastic bin with either a mains or battery-operated aerator. Experience has shown that if the seawater is kept cool, clean and well aerated, sandeels can be kept for months.

When freezing sandeels, freeze them in small packs so that wastage is kept to a minimum.

Live sandeels are best fished from a boat on a light leger rig with a long trace. The eel is hooked by passing the hook through the lower jaw and nicking the point through the tough rib of belly skin.

When shorefishing the eel has to withstand casting forces so it is best hooked through the tougher tail flesh with a turn or two of elasticated cotton taken around the wrist of the tail and the hook shank.

Mackerel are among the most versatile of all fish baits. They can be used whole for larger species, usually with the backbone removed so that the bait has movement. But the mackerel's main use is as a cutbait. It is filleted and further cut to hook size when the combination of oily flesh and tough shiny skin proves attractive to most species.

Mackerel is best purchased at the quayside where the freshest are most likely to be those caught from inshore handline boats which are rarely at sea for more than a day.

Fillet and cut the mackerel immediately into bait size pieces and freeze in small packs to provide just enough for occasional requirements.

Mackerel can be caught from the shore by spinning with a small, heavily-weighted silver spinner or by float fishing with a small sliver of silver-sided mackerel flesh as bait.

The traditional mackerel feathers are still the best from a boat but make sure a heavy sinker is used. The boat skipper will locate the shoal on an echo-sounder and without a heavy sinker the feathers will end up many yards downtide of the shoal. Give the feathers some movement by working the rod, or use the reel by reeling up and down through the shoal.

Herrings and pilchards can be cut into bait in the same manner as mackerel. These fish

When filleting and cutting mackerel for hook bait make sure that the knife is sharp. Neat cutting makes the bait both more attractive and more economical.

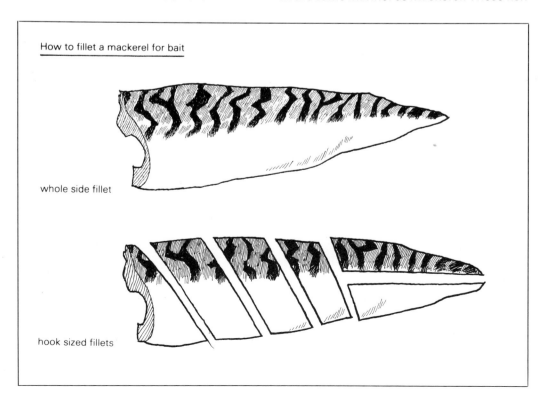

How to fillet a mackerel for bait

whole side fillet

hook sized fillets

are much softer in the flesh than mackerel so they need more care in their preparation and use, especially when casting. A few turns of elasticated cotton can be useful in keeping the bait properly presented on the hook.

Sprats are smaller, soft oily-fleshed fish which can be used whole, cut in half or filleted. They can be frozen in the same manner as mackerel. Baits are best prepared when the sprats are fresh and then frozen.

Squid and cuttlefish are not really fish but molluscs. For practical purposes, however, they can be classed as a 'fish' bait. The tough white flesh of the squid and cuttlefish is attractive to a large number of sea fish, but often used in conjunction with another soft bait to make a bait 'cocktail'.

Squid can be caught off the South West coast from September to Christmas but they are more usually purchased at the quayside or from a fishmonger.

Squid and cuttlefish are easily cut into bait-sized pieces and are particularly suitable for deep freezing. Small squid imported from America can be used whole or as a cut bait with the tentacles of large or small species making excellent hookbaits.

Crustacean baits

Prawns are an excellent bait and tend to be under-used except by those who know their full potential. They can be collected by pushing a handnet through the weeded fringes of rockpools but the bigger bait-sized specimens are more easily obtained in a dropnet worked around the sides of a pier, or better still, a fish quay where fishermen clean their catch.

Prawns are best kept alive in an aerated bucket or seawater aquarium. Alternatively, use a perforated container suspended below the surface in a quiet corner of the harbour.

They make a fine float-fished bait, used with a wire hook passed through the second or third segment of the tail. Dead prawns are a poor second best.

Crab baits

Shore and inshore boat anglers regard crabs as among the most effective and consistent of baits.

Squid is an excellent bait for most species of fish, especially winter cod. It is easy to cut into bait-sized pieces and can be used on its own or with another soft bait to make a bait 'cocktail'.

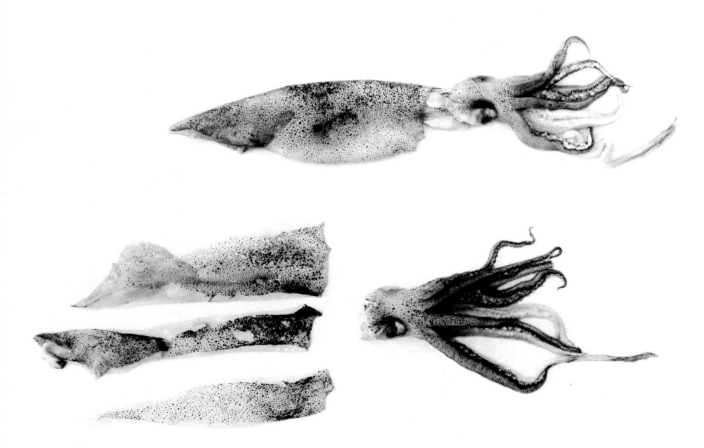

Above A peeler crab with its shell removed. They are best prepared for bait by removing legs, nippers and the old shell, which can be added as extra weight when the bait has been cast a few times.

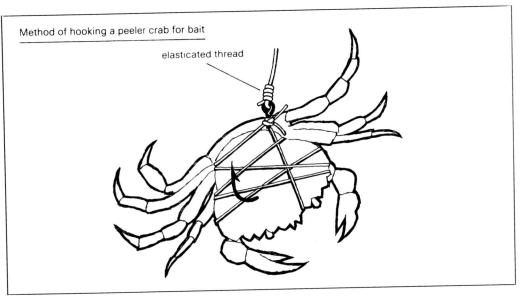

Method of hooking a peeler crab for bait

elasticated thread

All crabs can be baited in the same way as this hermit crab by threading them up the hook shank and then securing with a few turns of elasticated cotton.

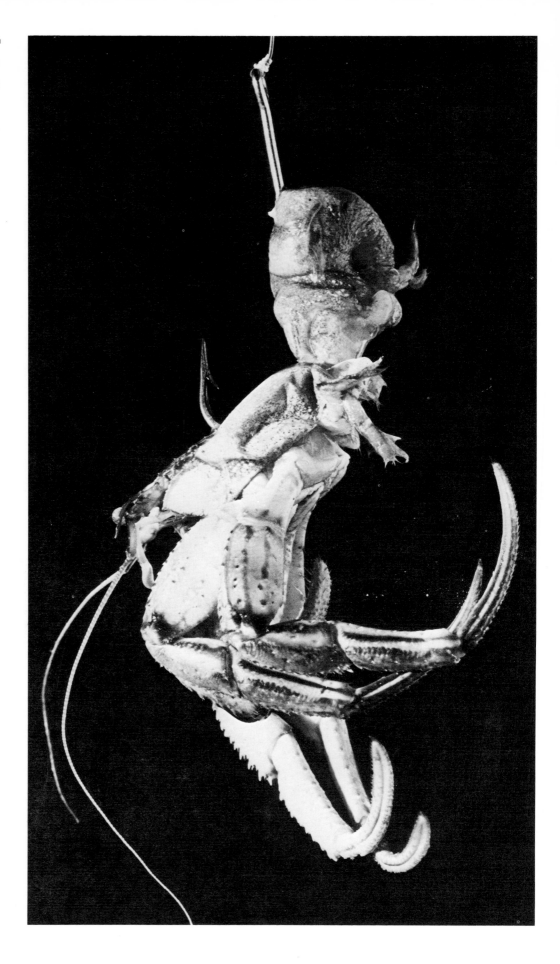

The crab has three distinct stages in its lifestyle. In its normal condition the shell is hard, and it is known as a hardback crab. When the crab has outgrown the shell and is ready for discard, it is a peeler crab. When the old shell is discarded the crab is in the vulnerable soft crab state.

Hardback crabs are not a lot of use for general fishing but there is one exception. Nothing is more likely to tempt a big ballan wrasse than a crunchy little hardback fished on a short strong paternoster.

Peeler crabs are not immediately recognisable but an easy way to determine whether a crab is a peeler is to press the shell firmly just above the rear legs. If the crab is a peeler the old shell will begin to lift away, revealing the soft new shell underneath. Before use, the old shell should be removed completely with the nippers and legs, saving them to add bulk to a bait that has been cast out once or twice. Larger peelers and 'softies' can be cut in half and, after hooking, tied into place with elastica-

ted cotton. Twist a small piece of wire around the eye of the hook to act as a spike to prevent the crab slipping down and bunching in the bend of the hook.

Softback crabs are instantly recognised by the soft leather-like texture of the back. Frequently a larger crab will carry a smaller female crab underneath its body. The female crab is always a peeler or 'softie' as mating can take place only during this moulting stage of the crab's evolution.

Crabs can be found by searching under rocks and seaweed near the low tide line. Peelers and softback crabs should be used as soon as possible. They can be frozen, but fresh crab is always better.

Keep peelers, 'softies' and hardbacks separate. They have no compunction about killing their own kind.

Hermit crabs are curious little creatures who take up residence in an empty whelk shell and make an excellent bait for many species of fish. These crabs are not found close inshore but are often washed up on beaches after a hard on-shore blow. An

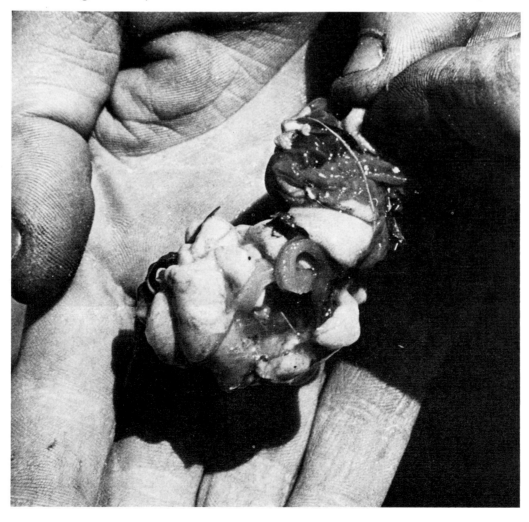

Five mussels securely trussed on a 4/0 hook with waste white cotton: a very effective bait.

arrangement with a commercial scollop dredger or inshore trawlerman will result in a few dozen being put to one side for you in the course of their activities. Usually used only fresh but can be kept for a few days in a large cool bait box.

Shellfish baits

Limpets are a bait to which few serious sea anglers attach much importance. They are useful only when stocks of more attractive baits are running low, particularly when fishing for wrasse when a piece of crab with a limpet to provide bulk can be a good bait. Limpets can be dislodged from rocks with a sudden sharp blow or by quick insertion of a thin blade between the rock and the limpet's shell.

Slipper limpets are also more useful as a standby bait and for adding bulk to crab or worm bait.

Mussels are held in high esteem as a bait in some areas. Larger mussels can be used as fresh bait but they are very soft-fleshed and a turn or two of elasticated cotton helps to hold them on the hook. Steaming them in a wire chip-frying basket firms up the flesh considerably without appearing to detract from their effectiveness as a fine bait.

Razorfish are probably the best of the shellfish baits with reasonably tough flesh that is attractive to a number of species, particularly flatfishes. They are often found in the same areas as black lugworm and reveal their position by a tell-tale keyhole-shaped entrance to a burrow. If you tread heavily there will be a spurt of water displaced upwards by the razorfish as it crash-dives.

They can be collected by digging or by pouring a handful of salt in the hole and

Species	Boat baits	Shore baits
Bass	Live and frozen sandeel, rag and lugworm, peeler and soft crab, squid, mackerel, prawn.	As for boat.
Bream (Red and Black)	Rag and lugworm, squid, mackerel, herring, pilchard, razorfish.	Worm or crab 'cocktails' with squid or mackerel.
Coalfish	Sandeel, ragworm, mackerel fillets, squid strip.	Sandeel, ragworm, mackerel strip, squid strip.
Cod	Lugworm, sandeel, ragworm, mackerel, squid, fish baits.	Lugworm, peeler crab, ragworm, squid, fish baits.
Conger	Mackerel, herring, pilchard, squid, small pouting, wrasse, bream.	Most fish baits.
Dabs	Small peeler crab, rag and lugworm, small mackerel and herring, squid.	As for boat but 'cocktails' favourite.
Dogfish	Mackerel, squid strip, most baits.	Almost any bait.
Flounder	Rag and lugworm, peeler crab, mussel, razorfish, small fish strips.	As for boat but best bait varies with locality.
Haddock	Rag and lugworm, mussel, razorfish, sandeel, prawn, mackerel, squid strip.	As for boat but best bait varies with locality.
Ling	Mackerel, herring, pilchard, squid.	Fish baits but rarely caught from shore.
Mackerel	Mackerel, pilchard, herring, squid strip, small sandeel or strip, feathers.	As for boat plus spinners.
Mullet	Small ragworm, fish flesh, bread.	As for boat.

washing it down with a sustained squirt of water from a liquid detergent bottle. Immediately the razor rises to the surface a spade is thrust into the sand to prevent its retreat.

Razorfish can be kept fresh for a few days if covered in damp sacking or seaweed. If to be frozen do it immediately, putting just a few in each polythene bag.

Thread razorfish flesh carefully on to a fine wire long-shanked hook with a little over the eye of the hook. A turn or two of elasticated cotton will prevent it sliding down and bunching in the bend of the hook.

Baits listed in this section cover only the essentials. A thinking, practical angler will retain an open mind and be prepared to press into service such seemingly exotic items as bacon rind or banana. If it works, use it!

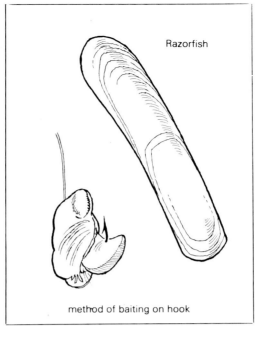

Razorfish

method of baiting on hook

Razorfish is one of the best shellfish baits, with reasonably tough flesh. When baiting up thread the razorfish carefully on to a fine long-shanked wire hook, with a little over the eye of the hook and a turn or two of elasticated cotton.

Species	Boat baits	Shore baits
Plaice	Live sandeel, mackerel and squid strip, rag and lugworm, razorfish, peeler crab.	As for boat. Best bait varies with locality.
Pollack	Live sandeel, fish and squid strips, ragworm.	As for boat.
Pouting	Rag and lugworm, mackerel, herring, squid strip, razorfish, mussel.	As for boat.
Ray (various)	Live sandeel, peeler crab, prawn, mackerel, herring, pilchard strip.	As for boat. Best bait varies with locality.
Shark	Whole mackerel, pilchard, herring.	Fish baits but rarely caught from shore.
Skate	Whole mackerel, herring.	Mainly caught from boats.
Sole	Rag and lugworm, peeler crab.	Rag and lugworm, peeler crab, worm and crab tipped with fish or squid 'cocktail'.
Tope	Fresh mackerel fillets, squid, whole small fish such as dabs, bream, pouting, whiting, plaice.	As for boat.
Turbot/Brill	Live sandeel, mackerel, herring fillets, sprats.	Fish baits. Occasional crab and worm.
Whiting	Mackerel, pilchard, herring, squid, sprat, rag and lugworm, mussel, razorfish.	Rag and lugworm, mussel, razorfish, crab, mackerel, herring, pilchard, squid strips.
Wrasse (Ballan)	Hardback and peeler crab, rag and lugworm, sometimes sandeel and fish strips.	Hardback and peeler crab, rag and lugworm; crab, worm, limpet 'cocktail'.

Casting styles

There is no magic involved in casting a bait over 125 yards. Anyone with reasonable co-ordination and average strength can do it with standard beach fishing tackle. The difference between good casters and the rest is that the man who gets his baits way out to sea has done his homework. He also catches more fish.

It is useless to go to the beach and thrash away with a rod in the hope that everything will suddenly fall into place and produce a 150 yard cast. The technique must be developed in a logical manner, progressing in easy stages from an off-the-ground cast to the more powerful pendulum cast. The best solution is personal tuition from a professional casting coach. Next best is to join forces with an experienced caster. The third option is to go out into a big field with a rod and reel and practise the easy exercises detailed later in this section.

Practise is a double-edged weapon. In reality, most angler's practice is a lottery. They think that if they stand there long enough the various factors will gel to produce good results. In fact, they perfect their mistakes.

When there is an understanding of what is trying to be done, practise takes a positive course. By concentrating only on what is correct, and by treading a clearly defined path to the goal, fast progress can be made and the time spent in the field is reduced to an hour or two a week. With care and commonsense, plus one or two professional lessons, a beginner can cast more than 100 yards within a day or two of first picking up a beach rod. In three months he can cast over 150 yards.

There is no precise formula for success but all casting styles are based on one over-riding principle of making the rod 'work', which means stressing it efficiently into its full compression curve and then releasing all the stored power to the weight. There is no more to casting than this, regardless of what tackle is used or which style is adopted. If the rod does not 'work', an angler will never cast well.

Shorefishing rods are discussed elsewhere in the book so there is no need to go farther into this topic here other than to underline the importance of butt stiffness and tip sensitivity in the rod blank and to say that nearly all anglers benefit from learning to cast with a 5 oz weight.

The first stage in any cast is to take up the inevitable slackness that exists in the line when the weight is just hanging from the rod tip. Second is the creation of tension in the rod, which means bending it against the inertia of the terminal tackle so that when the final spurt of arm power is applied, just before the line is released, the whole system is moving under moderate load and in precise order.

The target is smooth efficiency of body and tackle. Never allow over-exertion for sheer distance. It destroys the flow of the cast and produces a low, left flight path. Height is what to strive for; distance is a by-product.

Aim for easy height and the distinct feeling that the rod is doing the work. Think in terms of about 40° elevation being the ideal trajectory. If there is a common error in casting it is driving the weight up at an angle that is too shallow. Too much height is almost impossible to achieve when casting at full power; the more effort put in, the lower the cast becomes—almost automatically.

A bad cast happens with a heaving combination of straight rod, loose line and misplaced weight. Shovel in all the muscle you like but the cast will go nowhere. If the sequence is correct you finish by merely flicking over a fully-loaded rod which is pulling the weight along exactly the right path. The feeling of effort on a 120 yard cast is less than one-quarter of that required to thrash 75 yards any old style.

Be sure to cast consistently. The man who puts every cast straight down the field and each cast is within a few yards of the last eventually makes a better caster than he who scatters weights all over the field. Consistency, smoothness and full concentration are the hallmarks of the expert. Distance develops all by itself as you become familiar with the technique. Be realistic on distance. Tournament records exceed 240 yards but they are no yardstick for beach fishing. The man who drops his baits over the 150 yards mark is a rarity, even these days. That equals a no-bait distance of 200 yards.

Good casting starts at 100 yards with baits; 125 yards is excellent and 140 yards is truly expert. There are probably only 50 anglers in Britain who can regularly fish beyond 160 yards, even in perfect conditions. Tune the brain to reality. A cast of 150 yards without baits is fine. It takes sheer hard work to get much farther, with 200 yards casting probably a result of practice and a goodly measure of talent.

Basic off-the-ground cast

The aim is to produce a small amount of tension in the rod by pulling the weight off the ground. Then the rod is compressed by pushing and pulling with the arms so that upon release the sinker flies off at full power.

Stance and preparation. Tie the sinker to the end of the leader with a tucked half-blood knot. Adjust the line so that the weight hangs about 4 ft from the tip of the rod. Stand with toes on an imaginary line extending towards the target. Assuming you are right handed, now shift the left foot 6 inches back from the line so that the stance opens to bring the chest a little more square on to the target. This is a firm stance for power application.

Refer to diagram 1. Turn clockwise from the waist to face away from the casting direction. Flip the reel out of gear or pull back the bale arm. Swing the sinker away to the right of the imaginary line and drop it on the ground at the full extent of your reach. The right arm will now be straight and the rod will form an extension of it. The leader and sinker are also on that line. Hold the rod tip just clear of the ground. All this will place the left hand roughly in front of the face, perhaps as high as forehead level. Now turn the head around to look over the left shoulder towards casting direction. Body weight is on the right leg and the rod feels like a javelin in the right hand.

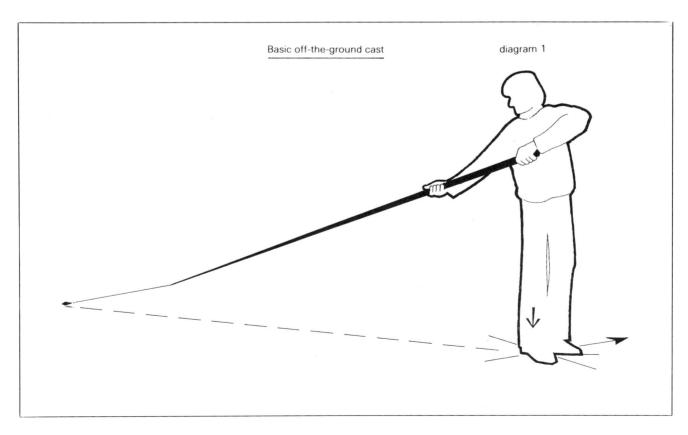

Basic off-the-ground cast   diagram 1

The initial pull (diagram 2). Concentrate your gaze on an imaginary patch in the sky at approximately 40° elevation and in line with the casting target. Gently draw on the rod butt with the right hand until you feel the slackness disappear from the leader. Now firmly, but smoothly, pull the rod forward and upward, javelin style. Let the left hand and elbow 'float' up and forward with the rod butt cap, as if you were about to prod the aerial spot with the cap. The left hand moves *high and well away from the body until the arm is straight*. This action automatically doubles up the right arm and brings the right hand close to the shoulder. Body weight naturally transfers to the left leg. The effect is to sweep the weight off the ground and to make the rod compress against the inertia of the lead.

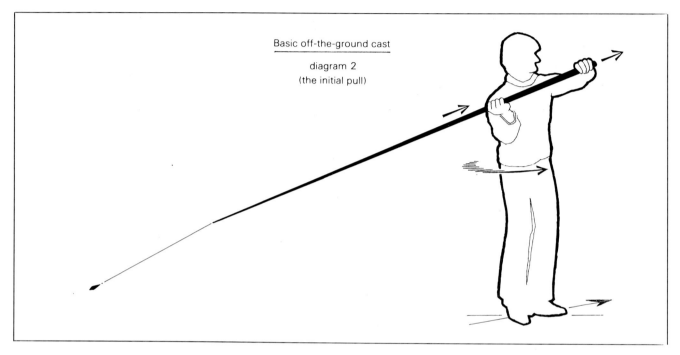

Basic off-the-ground cast

diagram 2
(the initial pull)

The final punch and pull (diagram 3). The gradual build-up of power makes the rod feel heavier and it seems its weigh is moving towards you from behind the right shoulder blade. As the left hand reaches full height and stretch, pull down with the left hand to guide the butt powerfully towards the bottom left of the rib cage. *At the same time punch the right hand up the intended line of flight.* The result is a smooth flick which turns the rod around an imaginary fulcrum on the butt halfway between the hands.

At the point of maximum power, release the line. You will almost certainly do that naturally and subconsciously. Unless there are severe errors of timing, which are extremely rare, make no attempt to control this stage of the cast. Just let it happen.

As the sinker flies through the air, hold the follow-through position and keep the rod high so that the line flows straight out of the tip ring. Stop the multiplier spool as soon as the weight hits the ground. On the fixed-spool, trap the line with your finger, then close the bale arm.

Practise this simple cast until you feel the rod beginning to function smoothly and with reasonable power. Fight against putting in brute force. A mere flick of the wrists sends the weight over 80 yards. The emphasis is on style, not distance. Extra effort can be added later and supplemented by using more body twist in the initial position: bring the leader and weight through an arc of 270° if you feel comfortable.

Recall the need to feel the rod coming from behind. This is important for the pendulum casts because it sets the body and the rod in the correct relationship to each other. It also prevents putting in too much power too soon which results in a low, left cast and a burned thumb.

The position of the head controls the 'shape' of the whole cast, its direction, smoothness and trajectory. Get the head into the right place by turning it to look at

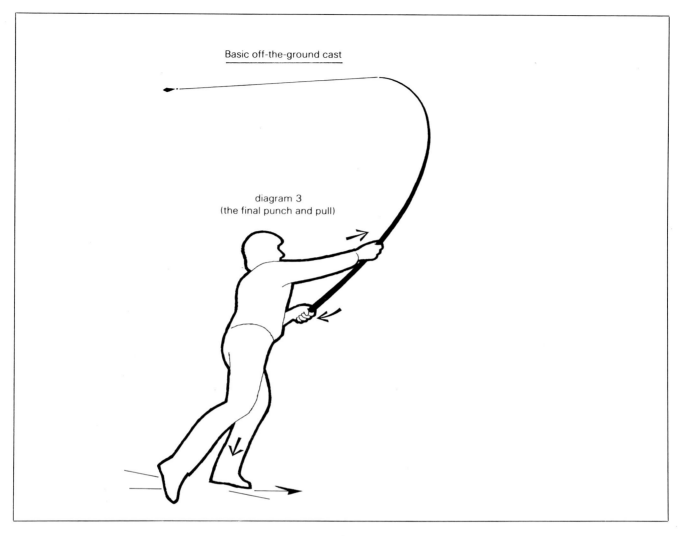

Basic off-the-ground cast

diagram 3
(the final punch and pull)

the aerial target just as soon as possible. If you are looking into the sky when the rod comes from behind your shoulder and moves into the punch-pull phase, the cast is virtually sure to be a good one. Fail to turn the head by, say, looking at either the reel or the weight means the power flow is distorted and wasted. So, to cast farther and more consistently, use your head . . . literally.

Adding the pendulum phase. The ground cast has all the essentials of successful casting. It may appear too simple to be worth practising but unless you can master the javelin-like pull follow-ed by the main arm action, time is wasted in progressing to more advanced casts. The aim is to cast 100 to 130 yards without baits, without over-runs and with absolute ease and confidence. Let's assume you can do that: why go any further into tech-nique?

The ground cast has limitations in prac-

tical fishing. Where the beach is flat and clean, lay out the terminal rig and leader just as you did in the field. Even a grip-wired sinker lifts off smoothly. But you are in trouble on a dirty beach, on a steeply shelving shingle and in the surf.

From a distance-casting aspect, the simple ground cast travels through an arc too small to develop maximum power. In addition, you can make the rod work more efficiently if it is compressed *before* you actually move it.

The pendulum style is the answer. It is more versatile, more powerful and, with expertise, smoother and less likely to cause over-runs. Virtually all top casters now use a variation of the basic pendulum cast and many rods are designed specifically for the technique.

Transition from the ground cast is easy enough if a few points are borne in mind. You *must* use a long drop between weight and rod tip so the pendulum swing is slow and extended. A drop of 7 ft is about right on an 11½ ft surf rod but you can increase this to 9 ft-plus in time. Also remember that power is applied late in the cast. It is no good thrashing into the pendulum swing itself. The sinker then hits the ground in mid-cast. Be sure to get your head around early, as you did before. Make certain the rod comes over from behind your right shoulder.

Pendulum cast

Initial pendulum swing (diagram 1). Take up the same foot position as before. Suspend the weight from a 7 ft drop. Throw the reel out of gear or pull back the bale arm. Twist the body clockwise until you feel coiled like a spring. This should bring the chest to face opposite the intended casting direction. Weight is on the right leg. Hold the rod vertical, at comfortable arms' length, and with the reel just above eye level. The sinker will hang close to the rod.

Refer to diagram 2. Imagine a line drawn at 45° to the right of the casting line. Push the rod tip and sinker away down that line. Do not let the rod fall below 30° elevation but make sure the sinker continues to swing outward in a pendulum arc which rises well above eye level.

When the sinker stops in mid-air, pull back on the rod to generate enough power to swing the sinker towards the right hand side of the rod, quickly past it and then up in the air behind your right shoulder. The sinker reaches maximum height on the inswing and then slows at the peak of the swing. At that moment, you will feel a distinct pause.

Refer to diagram 3. When you feel the pause, *gently* guide the rod down to the position used to start the ground cast. This time, however, the rod will already be under compression and the sinker will fly down into the correct path behind it.

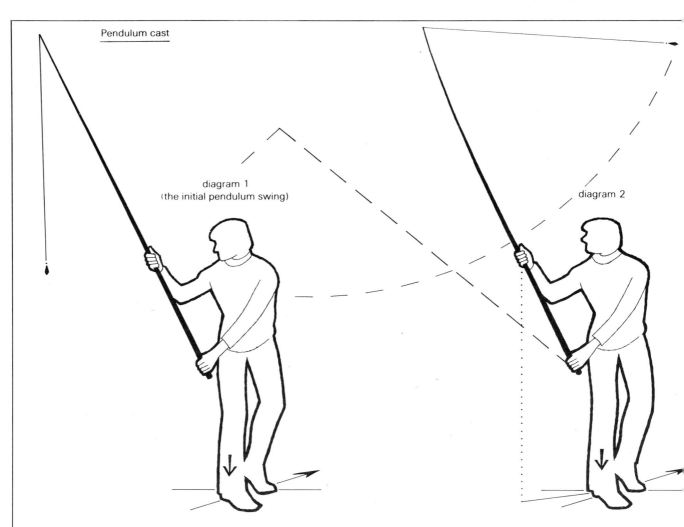

Pendulum cast

diagram 1
(the initial pendulum swing)

diagram 2

Neither rod tip nor sinker will hit the ground if the pendulum arc was correct and the drop between tip and sinker are long enough.

Turn your head to face the casting direction. You will feel the rod tense and grow heavier. At that point, swing through into the javelin pull then the punch-pull of the arms. Let the line release itself and then follow through as before (*diagram 4*).

Advanced casting

The techniques described in this section are intended to help a beginner to produce reliable 125 yard results with baits. The casts are nowhere near the most powerful but do not require specialised tackle or athletic performance.

The path beyond 150 yards is rugged. Very few anglers are prepared to dedicate themselves that much to the sport. There are thousands of anglers who want to be good casters but only a minority accept the burden of learning. It means hard work, regular practise and expense. There are no short-cuts.

There is no substitute at this intermediate point for either professional coaching or for working with other equally determined casters. A great deal is learned by watching top men in action so attend tournaments. When the 'shape' and power flow of a full-blooded cast is seen life is much easier. There is a clear mental picture of what you want to perfect. It is very hard to work towards something you have never seen. Whatever happens, look, ask and practise — these are the keys to high-class casting in distance and style from beach and tournament court.

The pendulum cast is deservedly most popular among top casters because it preserves most of the fishing characteristics of the rod. The majority of anglers prefer an 11½-12 ft rod for this work. A 200-yard rod is necessarily powerful and stiff in the butt

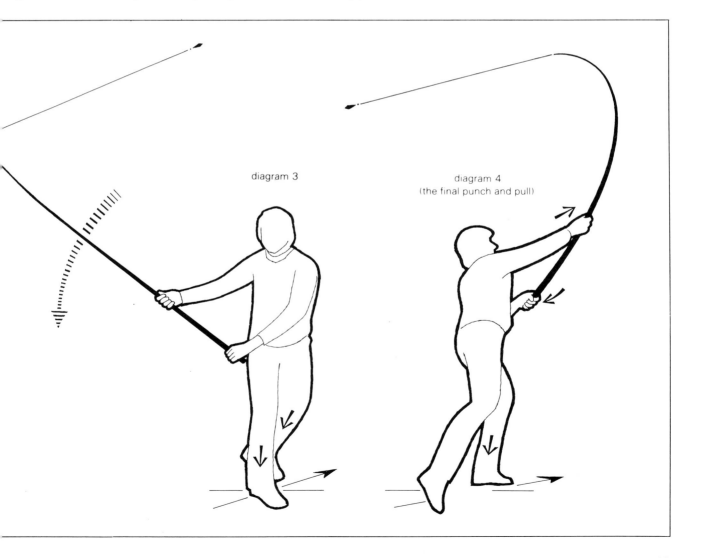

diagram 3

diagram 4
(the final punch and pull)

but can be reasonably light and sensitive for the beach.

The cast gains its enormous power when the casting arc is increased almost to 360°. The caster coils right up and the pendulum swing takes the sinker way over his head. The power flow starts early, while the body is still turned away from the sea. When the rod is pulled into position for the final punch, the sinker is moving fast and the rod is compressed fully. It is a beautiful cast to watch but can be a nightmare to learn unless the basics of the sport are already understood.

The full pendulum is the forte of the athletic man who relies as much on speed as on sheer strength to generate sufficient tip speed on the relatively short rod. Top pendulum casters tend to be the racehorse breed: long-limbed, loose and fast.

Anglers built on carthorse lines — very strong but quite slow-moving — excel at the back cast technique. This works on the theory that as much tip speed is generated on a long rod moved slowly as on a short rod moved quickly. Back, shoulders and arms do the work; the arms mainly guide the rod through the necessary arc. Where the emphasis of pendulum casting is a forward push, that of the back cast is a tractor-like pull.

Imagine tossing coal over your shoulder with a long-handled shovel. That is the broad principle of the back cast. The sinker is swung pendulum style behind the caster, who stands back to the sea, then is swept round with full force by a backward rotation of the body. The action is slow but immensely powerful, which permits a 14 ft-plus rod to be handled with ease. The cast also comes into its own with heavy weights with 8 oz leads no strain at all.

Fixed-spool and multiplier reels

Essentially, there is no difference in action between casting with fixed-spool or multiplier reels, other than the way the line is held before release. As releasing the line is generally a subconscious action, timing is less of a problem than might be imagined. Anglers who cast well can use either with absolute ease.

Fixed-spools are far more tolerant of error. Relying on their handling to compensate for your own failings means that a change to a multiplier will prove disastrous, as a multiplier's demand for smoothness will catch you out on your first cast.

However, multiplier anglers have no trouble in changing to fixed-spool reels because they have already achieved the necessary technique to iron out jerks. It is always the fixed-spool man who suffers, not because the multiplier is particularly fierce but because he cannot cast too well in the first place. If he worked on style, the distances would improve on the fixed-spool as well.

Fixed-spools offer tremendous advantages with light lines. With a line below 12 lb, the fixed-spool outcasts the multiplier and will more easily penetrate wind and tide. Whatever the conditions you can always put full power into a fixed-spool cast but a sure recipe for an over-run with a multiplier is to cast hard into a headwind without using a lot of brake.

Most back casters use a fixed-spool all the time. The reel is fitted low down on the butt, which helps counterbalance the rod weight. It is physically impossible for many casters to use a multiplier with this style, anyway, due to the lack of control. The fixed-spool has no drawbacks here and is particularly effective because the length of leader between reel and sinker is great enough to cushion the finger against cuts and burns. It is no wonder that back casters do well in fixed-spool tournament events as the rod, reel and technique blend perfectly.

Controlling a multiplier reel

Reels without centrifugal brakes. Plain reels are easy to use if they are tuned properly. The spool should run fast enough not to reduce the casting distance, but not so fast as to lose control. Most important, never cram on as much line as the spool can take. Keep the level to around $\frac{3}{16}$ inch down from the top and, if necessary, reduce it further. Indeed, there is some advantage in deliberately underfilling the reel at first. With only 150 yards of line on the spool, most reels are absolutely docile.

Correct lubrication is the second line of defence. The viscosity of the oil provides a fluid brake. Begin with a thick, fairly sticky oil such as 90 grade axle oil. This should reduce over-runs to the minimum; but if casting is poor, ultra-viscous STP additive oil will bind the reel still more. When confidence is gained, change down to 20-50 engine oil. This is normally as thin as you dare go for reliable casting but for maximum distance in practice sessions it

may help to thin it just a fraction with sewing machine oil. Neat sewing machine oil is far too thin for most casters and will make the reel over-run every cast.

Try to avoid tightening the left-hand bearing cap on reels such as the Penns which do not have a brake insert in the cap. Mitchells and Newells can be tightened down a little, but ideally the spool should have a very slight amount of end play on the spindle.

Reels with centrifugal brakes. Do not overload the spool but do keep the line fairly well up to the rim. Lubricate the bearings with 20-50 engine oil or even machine oil. Set the left-hand bearing to zero brake (see the reel instructions on how to do this). Insert the largest brake blocks into the centrifugal system and start casting. The big blocks will eliminate over-runs and will also savagely reduce casting range. If you do get over-runs, your technique is dreadful!

Change down to the next smallest blocks and practise again. If there is no problem in control, plus an improvement in distance, change down again. On most reels, you are now casting on the smallest blocks provided. The reel should stay in perfect control with distances increasing by around 15 per cent. Remain with that state of tuning until happy with the casting technique. Then take out one block at a time until left with just one small block in the reel. This is normally the best compromise between safety and maximum distance but requires a reasonably smooth technique.

Reel position

Beach reels are either fitted high on the butt and controlled with the right hand, or low down and operated with the left. There are advantages and snags with each position. Ideally, learn ambidextrous casting.

High position works well with multipliers and fixed-spool reels on 11-12 ft rods cast pendulum style. Longer rods benefit from having the reel at the butt because the balance and leverage are improved considerably. However, it is tiring to fish with a multiplier at the bottom of the rod; the up-rod hand still has to guide line on to the reel so it cannot be held far enough up the butt to create a good leverage. There is no such problem with a fixed-spool.

The reel at the butt makes the rod feel softer and smoother in action. You may well cast a lot further this way so try it and see. Rod length can be increased a little, which may also add distance to the cast, and there is far less likelihood of burning a thumb on the reel when the rod comes under full load.

Back casters must use the reel at the butt because a high position is physically impossible to exploit. The fixed-spool being the reel of choice, there are no weaknesses on the retrieve.

Rod length

Marginal alterations to rod length will affect the cast, with 11-12 ft rods ideal for beginners and perfectly acceptable for most beach fishermen of any capability. But do not be blind to the possibility of gaining a few yards by adding to the rod or even by cutting it down. Experiment carefully as an inch or two can also ruin your fishing. Remember that the long rod used on the practice field may be a menace on a sloping beach. Rods over 13 ft long are definitely suspect in this respect, except for back casters. Here, rod lengths up to 14 ft are common on the beach. Even so, many highly experienced tournament casters prefer 13-13½ ft rods for everyday beach work. Never over-gun yourself.

Thin machine oil is fine for lubricating casting reels if you are using brake blocks, otherwise expect over-runs.

Basic boat fishing tackle and rigs

Rods

Fibreglass is the material now used exclusively in the manufacture of boat rods. Two types are available, solid and hollow-glass. The former first appeared on the British angling scene around 1948 and soon began to replace conventional split cane. The new rods were much stronger, had a better action and, above all, were cheap to make. Solid glass is still with us in what the fishing tackle industry describe as 'boys' and holiday rods'.

A massive step forward in sport-fishing technology was achieved with the hollow-glass rod. This is produced from glass fibre cloth, which is wrapped tightly around a tapered tube called a mandrel. Bound with a form of Sellotape it is then hung in an oven where great heat melts the layers of cloth into one. After cooling the core is removed, leaving a hollow tube and the process of turning the blank into a fishing rod can now begin.

Manufacturers have a large number of mandrels, each one finely made with the correct taper. The amount of glass cloth placed on it determines the strength of the finished blank, which is called test curve.

The procedure has been simply described here but in reality great care must be taken, particularly during baking. If the temperature is incorrect, or varies, the finished blanks could have a flaw and ultimately break under pressure.

The quality of the glass cloth, how it is put on the mandrel and the resins used also play a vital part. The latest development combines glass fibre and carbon fibre in a highly technical process that produces a blank of incredible strength and lightness which is superior to carbon fibre on its own. Glass fibre and mixed carbon rods are unaffected by strong sunlight or the action of salt water. Being virtually unbreakable they have brought a new dimension to rod and line angling.

Lengths and fittings. A boat rod should not be shorter than $6\frac{1}{2}$ ft. A rod of this length must have five rings plus the tip ring, which is either a conventional eye or a roller. The roller is a big advantage on a rod being used for deep-water fishing against heavy species such as conger and ling, as line friction is considerably reduced at the point where it is greatest.

If it is to perform correctly, the roller must turn easily and should be wiped dry after each trip and well-oiled. A famous name for roller rings is *Aftco* which are fitted to most of the rods used in big game fishing. Some top quality rods have roller rings throughout, primarily to permit the use of wire line. The most common type of ring for a boat rod is of hard chrome which stands up extremely well to the cutting effect of monofilament line. Many new rods coming on to the fishing tackle scene feature speed guides which are rings lined with a very tough material which minimises friction.

Winch fittings. The importance of securely clamping the reel to the rod cannot be over-stressed. There is nothing worse than a reel slopping about from side to side when under pressure during the playing of a large fish. Some reels, usually from 4/0 upwards, have additional seat clamps with wing nuts, which give complete security. Most of the bars are far too long and should be sawn off to suit the diameter of the reel seats on rods to which the reel will be matched. The latest type of snap lock reel seats are also recommended. These allow a quick change to be made and are very positive in use.

This Welsh angler demonstrates the need for a strong harness as he bends into a large conger. The harness holds the rod butt secure allowing for arm movement and leaving the hands free to grip the rod more effectively.

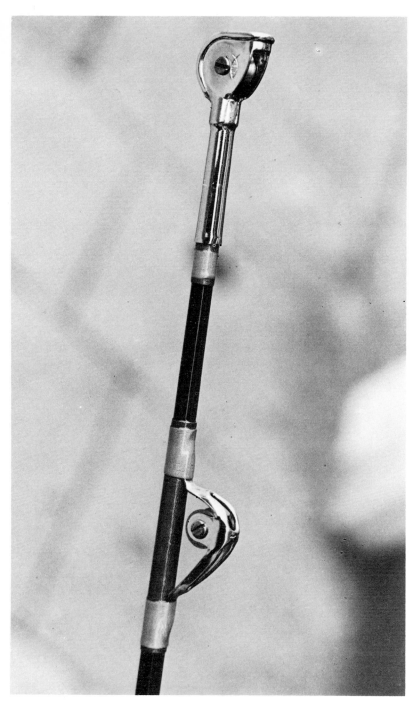

Boat rod classes. The International Game Fish Association, which has its base in the U.S.A., lays down certain rules concerning classes for World Record fish. Unfortunately, this organisation does little for European anglers fishing in their own waters as, with the exception of sharks and coalfish, all the 60 or so species listed are found on the Atlantic coast of the United States, or in the warmer seas of the world.

Pressure has been brought to bear on the Association for the inclusion of the conger eel, to name just one fish common to the waters this side of the Atlantic, but to date, little progress has been made. IGFA is, however, a very common set of initials in British boat fishing as manufacturers produce rods to conform to classes laid down by the Association, namely the 6, 12, 20, 30, 50, 80 and 130 lb tests. English-based manufacturers do produce rods in the heaviest category but these are for export and have no place in UK boat fishing with the exception perhaps of bluefin tuna, a sport formerly enjoyed off Scarborough in the North Sea. There is a growing interest once again in this great sporting species and the foreseeable future could witness a revival in new areas.

An 80 lb test rod, however, is really the heaviest needed in the waters around this country for use against porbeagle, mako, thresher shark and common skate. In truth, the 50 lb test rod is sufficient for shark as it is a free swimming mid-water species with no ambition to sulk close to bottom hazards. This weight of rod fits conger fishing very well, provided it has good lifting power in the butt, combined with a reasonable degree of flexibility. In the past, rods often described as being ideal for congering were quite unsuitable, most being far too stiff to allow a large fish to be played out. It is the spring of a rod that

Above A rod with roller rings is a big advantage for deep-water fishing against heavy species of fish, such as conger and ling, because friction is much reduced.

Right The most popular method of fitting the reel to the rod is with this screw fitting which is very secure.

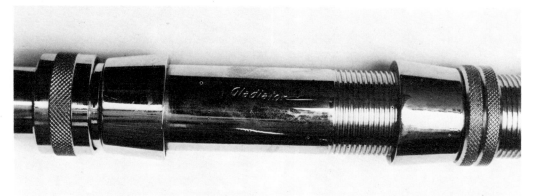

eventually tires the fish and wins the game for the angler.

Fortunately, a gradual awareness of what constitutes a suitable rod has resulted in major manufacturers producing excellent models. In turn, deep-water anglers have realised the benefit to be gained from using lighter tackle and there is a definite swing to 30 lb class outfits, even for wreck fishing. A 30 lb class rod can handle up to $1\frac{1}{2}$ lb of lead, the size often needed when fishing deep water.

Next on the list is the 20 lb test rod which fits the bill for general boat fishing. Among the species caught with it are red and black bream, coalfish, pollack, whiting, pouting, dogfish, ray and most of the flatfish tribe. Weights up to 12 oz may be used, which limits fishing to medium runs of tide. In stronger tides 30 lb tackle should be brought back into service.

Although not in the IGFA list of classes, 15 lb test rods are becoming increasingly popular. A 10-ft model now available in Britain is near perfect for many free-swimming species such as bass and pollack and is a rod for bottom-feeders like whiting, codling, spurdog and bream.

A relative newcomer to the British boat fishing scene is the 12 lb class rod which, quite rightly, has quickly found popularity with many dedicated saltwater men. It offers ultra-sensitivity, which is a great asset when trying to lure shy fish to the hook. A rod like this can make the difference between a blank day and a fine creel of fish and its value in general boat fishing cannot be overstated.

Last of all is the 6 lb test, a specialist class if there ever was one. Light tackle experts working our waters have made incredible catches including shark weighing nearly 100 lb. In fairness to others this type of fishing must be done on trips specifically organised for the purpose of light tackle sport. Even a moderate-sized fish hooked on a 6 lb rod takes a long time to bring to the net and it is grossly unfair to anglers who have paid for a conventional charter trip to be messed about by a selfish individual bent on achieving some fishing miracle on a wand of a rod and fine line. It is happening all too frequently. Sheer skill must be linked with commonsense but unfortunately this is not always the case.

Multiplying reels

Most boat anglers use a multiplying reel

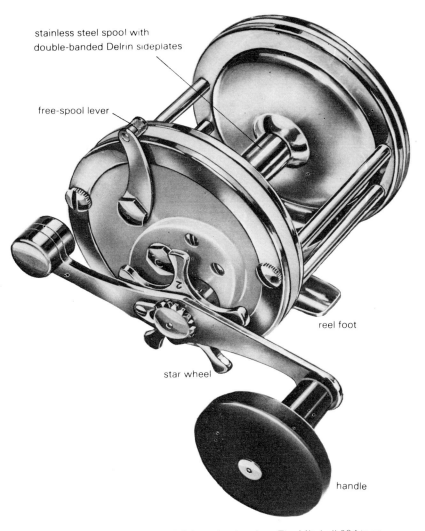

stainless steel spool with double-banded Delrin sideplates

free-spool lever

reel foot

star wheel

handle

The Mitchell 624 is an immensely strong big capacity boat reel, suitable for all deep-water and wreck fishing.

with a metal spool for fishing in both shallow and deep water. This type of reel is designed to retrieve line rapidly and has ratios between 2-1 and 5-1. In simple terms, for every complete revolution of the winding handle, the gearing revolves the drum the appropriate number of times, e.g. five times in the 5-1.

In recent years, reels with automatic gearing have become popular, with ratios ranging from $2\frac{1}{2}$-1 to $4\frac{1}{2}$-1 and in a few cases 5-1. They change down into low gear when a fish is being pumped and into a high gear when only the line and end tackle is recovered. The normal size of multiplier for general boat fishing is about 4/0 but wreck fishing for heavier species demands a 6/0. Another useful feature on some models is an inbuilt digital counter which accurately records and displays the footage of line that is out. This is very useful when fishing in deep water. Some multipliers up to 4/0 have a rotating or bar type line distributor which lays retrieved line evenly across the width of the spool.

Multipliers feature a star or lever drag which allows a fish to take line without the handles revolving. Cheap models have a variety of shortcomings and invariably suffer from stripped gearing when used in deep-water fishing against weighty specimens. It is always sound policy to buy the best reel you can afford. This will pay off handsomely in the long term.

Top quality multipliers incorporate aircraft bearings in the end plates which give the spool an even action and reduce friction to a minimum. Lever-drag multipliers are in the top flight and can set you back a pretty penny but are well worth the extra money. The lever does away with the on-off mechanism necessary in conventional multipliers and the amount of drag placed against a fish can be altered precisely while it is played. Lever-drag reels are perfect for all forms of bottom fishing, pirking, and trolling.

A centre-pin reel is simply a revolving drum with one or two winding handles. It does not generally feature any form of clutch mechanism and when a running fish demands line, it has to be given with the palm of the hand acting as a brake. This requires a level of skill if knuckles are not to suffer a severe rap from the handles which move with the spool. Fishing without a slipping clutch puts the angler in direct contact with the fish and every movement it makes is transmitted to the fingers. Centre-pins are not in wide use although several types are manufactured. The average width of the drum is between 4 and 6 inches and made of metal or plastic.

Giant wooden reels known as 'starbacks', some with a diameter of 15 inches, exist. These have a fantastic rate of retrieve and are used by a few specialists fishing very deep water off the Northern Isles and in competitions where the capture of large numbers of fish very quickly is the criteria.

This type of large centre-pin must not be confused with those still found on Cornish shark fishing boats. These are the classic Hardy Fortunas, perhaps the Rolls Royce

Multiplier reels fitted with a lever drag are usually both expensive and of the highest quality. They normally are used in big game fishing but are also perfect for bottom fishing, pirking and trolling as the amount of drag placed against a fish can be altered precisely while it is played.

of all boat reels, which went out of manufacture over 20 years ago. The Fortuna was made in a range of sizes, the seven-inch, weighing $5\frac{1}{2}$ lb being the most commonly used. It features a silk-smooth movement and a brass star drag second to none. Two-inch handles give all the leverage an angler could ask for. Unlike the large game fishing multipliers, which are fished on top of the rod creating certain problems of balance, the centre-pin hangs below in a conventional way and is really more pleasant to use. Line capacity is anything up to 750 yards of 60 lb braided and a third more in monofilament. Once heard, the sound of line being ripped off a Fortuna by a running porbeagle or blue shark is never forgotten.

Lines

Most sea fishing is done with monofilament lines available in a multitude of breaking strains. It has an amazing strength to diameter ratio, which cuts down considerably on the amount of lead needed to hold bottom in deep water when there is a fast run of tide. Cheap monofilament is best avoided as it is often suspect in strength and very springy. Top quality 'mono' is made to a specification which produces an extremely smooth and pliable line, usually as close to the stated breaking strain as makes no difference. It has great durability and abrasion resistance and ties well with high knot strength.

Monofilament line comes in a variety of colours, natural white, blue and gold are the most popular and there is not much to choose between them when it comes to visibility in water. There is a continual search for a line that fish cannot see.

True, monofilament stretches under pressure and this to some extent does have a detrimental effect on the setting of a hook in the fish's mouth. The problem is overstated but the stretch is an inbuilt safety factor against the run of a large specimen.

Braided lines. Dacron and Terylene lines are not suitable for general sea fishing, particularly bottom legering. They are greatly increased in diameter, even in low breaking strains, and their absorption of water demands the use of at least double the amount of lead needed for a comparable weight of monofilament. In water over 20 fathoms deep it takes only a moderate tide run to put a huge bow in the line, which places the angler out of direct touch

with the quarry. The material is also easily damaged by contact with rough ground and the rusting ironwork of wrecks. Braided lines are perfectly acceptable for shark fishing, but at least a 6/0 multiplier is needed to carry enough yardage for 'blues' and a 9/0 for the much larger porbeagle.

Wire. The use of wire by sea angling specialists is growing but many are still unaware of its benefits. It is the complete answer to bottom fishing in deep water and fast tides as very small weights can be used. The angler is always in direct contact with the terminal tackle and every bite is transmitted powerfully to the rod. But the use of wire does require certain tackle and disciplines. Ideally, the rod should be soft in action with roller rings throughout or guides lined with aluminium oxide which is tough enough to resist the cutting effect of the wire. Multipliers with wide spools and line levellers are unsuitable for fishing with this material. A narrow spool model with a large diameter and capacity for 300 yards of 36 lb wire is ideal. This specification fits the Penn Master Mariner or Super Mariner, both of which have a very fast retrieve ratio. Centre-pins can be used with wire but the problems with this type of reel, as already detailed, should be taken into consideration.

Wire line must be fished positively at all times and allowed to run down to the bottom under tension. Failure on this point will result in a mass of coils and kinks which can never be straightened. Leaving the rod resting on the gunwale with the line in the water while enjoying a sandwich is just not on! Wire must always be used in association with a monofilament trace with the wire twisted around itself with pliers after being passed through the eye of the swivel or link. It is essential to snip off the end cleanly. A pair of leather gloves should always be handy to assist in breaking out. If a hang up occurs never tackle it with bare hands.

Hooks

There are hundreds of different hook patterns but sea anglers need concern themselves with only a few. Among the most useful is the long-shanked Aberdeen, which is extremely fine in the wire, needle-sharp and the perfect combination for live-baiting sandeel and prawn. This hook is popular for estuary and tidal river dinghy

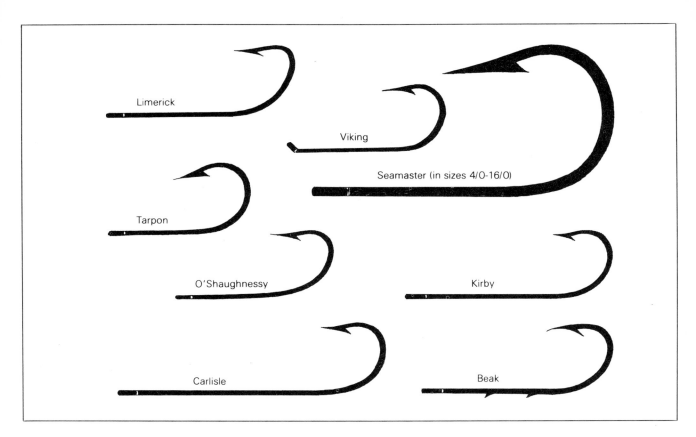

Common hook patterns used by the boat fisherman: the Beak has bait-holding nicks; the Limerick and O'Shaughnessy are general purpose patterns; the Tarpon and Viking are good all rounders; the Carlisle is for flat fishing; the Kirby is a good pattern for tying mackerel and cod flies; and the Seamaster is a big game hook.

fishing for bass, flounder, dabs and plaice but is equally good for offshore work against large pollack and bream. No tackle box is well-equipped without a range of Aberdeens between size 1 and 4/0.

For general bottom fishing two types stand out. The Limerick is well-suited for paternoster use, its pull being direct and with excellent penetration. A good hook for legering is the O'Shaughnessy, which features a wide gape between the point and the shank and is very strong and ideal for holding heavy fish such as conger and ling. A hook needs to be big and tough for a prolonged encounter with an eel's powerful jaws and to carry a big bait. For wreck fishing, there's none better than a forged eye Seamaster, ranging in size from 9/0 to 12/0, which is connected to a couple of feet of cable laid wire. No matter how much pressure this kind of hook receives it will not straighten as a conventional conger hook is prone to do. For reef conger fishing an O'Shaughnessy with a twisted eye is adequate.

Bait-holder hooks with a number of slices in the shank to prevent a bait slipping down to the bend are popular, but have disadvantages. Of necessity, the wire is thick which gives only moderate penetration, worms are ripped to pieces by the sharp edges and the strength of the shank is considerably reduced.

The hook is the one item of tackle that is in direct contact with the fish but often receives scant attention. Cheap hooks are brittle, poorly finished and often quite unsuitable for the task they are asked to perform. They should not be dumped in a tackle box and allowed to take on a film of rust but kept in a dry state or wrapped in a piece of cloth dipped in pilchard oil.

Hooks should be checked for a turned point or dullness before being cast out and after each retrieve. A soft stone moistened with oil should always be handy to hone a point to maximum sharpness. Any that show signs of real wear must be discarded. Failure to observe this simple rule could lose a good fish.

Leads

Float work and drift-lining from a small dinghy requires split shot, ball and barrel leads. Fishing in deep water in spring tide periods needs up to 3 lb of lead to hold the bait on the bottom. For this reason charter skippers usually drift-fish during new and full moon periods. It is well to remember this when booking a deep-water fishing trip as working on the drift can be a hard and tiring business.

Paternosters can be taken down with bombs or torpedoes and it is wise to have a selection from 6 oz to 2 lb. The same types are used in conjunction with wire boom rigs for long-trace single-hook fishing, but rarely heavier than 12 oz as the bait is fished off the bottom.

Leads for legering must have a large diameter base. The cone is the best type but grip leads do an adequate job. Leger leads can be rigged with a rotten bottom by tying a small swivel to the eye with light nylon which is then run on to the reel line. If the weight becomes jammed, pulling will break the line and free the trace. This is a big help when expensive wire rigs are being used.

Trolling for bass and pollack is a popular and often rewarding way of fishing. The size of lead depends very much on the strength of tide, speed of the boat and how deep the fish are running. To get a bait well down a 1 lb lead is often needed and for shallow water fishing use 8-12 oz leads. Trolling leads should have a centre of gravity below the level of the line, which prevents any suggestion of spinning providing the swivels mounted behind and in front of the weights are working correctly.

Large Jardines, which are mounted by running the reel line in a groove, are widely used in this form of fishing as they can be changed very quickly without cutting the line if a heavier or lighter one is required.

Pirks and jiggers are now established methods of fishing over wrecks for pollack, coalfish, ling and cod. They come in all weights from 4 oz to 26 oz and in many different shapes. Pirks made up from car door handles and sections of chrome-plated tube cut from pram handles do catch fish but do not work as well as the professionally-designed, manufactured article. The best shapes flutter as they are worked to represent a swimming fish. They are available in chrome and a variety of colours with some covered in Flectolite, a material borrowed from the jewellery industry. This reflects all the colours of the spectrum. Pirks can be baited with strips of squid or mackerel. Coloured streamers attached to the treble hook give added attraction.

Factory-made leads are expensive. The alternative is to buy diecast aluminium moulds and scrap lead from a metal merchant and make your own. The initial outlay for a complete set of moulds to

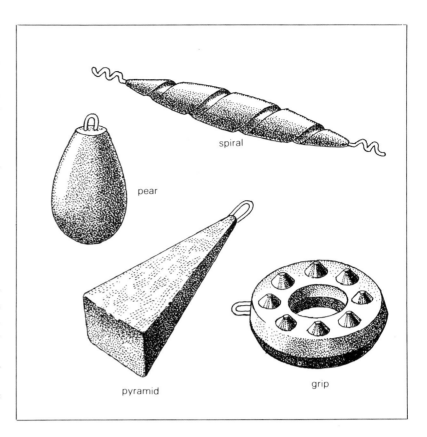

make leads between 2 oz and 8 oz, and a bag of grip wire, will be about £15. The price of lead varies constantly but £5 will buy enough to make several dozen leads of various sizes at a unit cost considerably less than a shop price.

Lead weights should be made in a shed or garage, never in a kitchen. Moulds must be absolutely dry or the molten metal will spit dangerously when it strikes the aluminium. Lead pipe should be cut into small pieces and melted in an iron ladle over a paraffin or gas blowlamp. When ready for use the metal is poured slowly into the block which is best gripped lightly in a vice. After allowing a few minutes for the lead to set the mould can be removed, split open and the weight dropped to one side. After a dozen or so leads have been made, the block becomes extremely hot and must be left to cool for at least ten minutes. Gloves and protective goggles should be worn. Children should *not* attempt these processes without expert adult supervision.

Swivels – Links

There are many varieties of swivel and all of them have an important place in sea fishing. The most common is the plain barrel, which is simply a body and two twisted

A selection of some of the more common weights used in boat angling.

wire eyes which revolve independently of each other on small heads of metal. Although mass-produced by the million the engineering is to fine tolerances to ensure the swivel performs its primary function of preventing line from twisting. This type of basic swivel is made in many sizes to cater for different techniques and species. Each has a corresponding number, as is given to hooks. For example, 1/0, 3/0 or 5/0. There is a tendency for too large a swivel to be used in general sea fishing. This is quite unnecessary as the strength of a small swivel is many times greater than the reel line that could be employed. The three-way swivel used for paternosters is a direct extension of the barrel. The basic swivel is available with a snap and spring link attachment for connecting a trace, line or lure. This type is also useful as a weight carrier, particularly in conjunction with wire boom rigs, which are described later.

Other derivatives of the barrel swivel include the buckle and the very safe corkscrew link, used in a variety of ways as trace and line connectors.

Top quality heavy duty swivels, such as the box type, should be used when fishing for shark, skate and conger.

Salt water quickly corrodes so swivels should be checked before use to ensure that the eyes turn freely. Large swivels fixed permanently to wire traces must be given a wipe of pilchard oil.

Booms

Wire and sea fishing have always gone together but far too much emphasis is put on wire as a means of keeping the hook and line apart. All too often wire booms are used in paternosters but just add a complication to what is basically a simple rig that can be tied from a single piece of nylon as described in the section dealing with tackle rigs. A stainless steel French boom, generally 9 inches long, is the basis for the 'flying collar'. This is a unique rig developed in the West of England for pollack and coalfish fishing and enables a trace up to 20 ft long to be worked without fear of tangling with the reel line, provided there is a reasonable run of tide.

The rig is made up by attaching split rings to all three corners of the boom.

The most important function of the swivel or link is to prevent line from twisting. To ensure that they work properly it is necessary to check them frequently; a wipe of pilchard oil will keep corrosion down to a minimum.

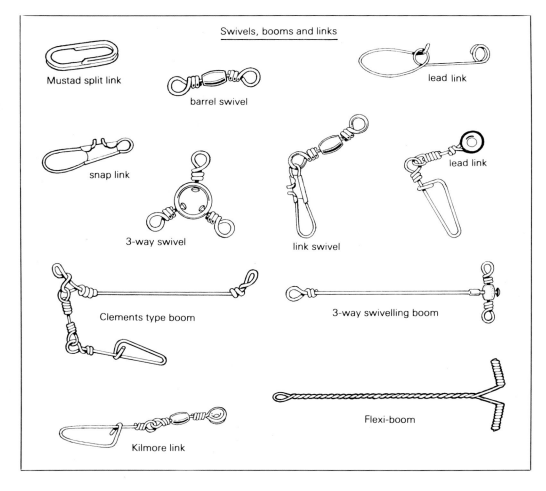

Swivels, booms and links

Mustad split link

barrel swivel

lead link

snap link

3-way swivel

link swivel

lead link

Clements type boom

3-way swivelling boom

Flexi-boom

Kilmore link

These carry barrel swivels at two points and a swivelled weight holder at the third (see diagram). The reel line and the trace are connected to the barrel swivels and a weight, which can be changed quickly to suit individual tidal conditions, to the swivelled weight holder. A manufactured plastic sea boom on the same principle, but without the swivels, is available in tackle shops but is far too short to carry the very long trace. There is absolutely no substitute for the French or similar L-shaped boom for top class 'flying collar' fishing.

Booms for legering include Kilmore and Clements. These are basically weight carriers placed on the reel line and free to slide, allowing a fish to take line without feeling the weight. Kilmore is a single-eyed boom, which means the average 2-inch long weight dangles approximately 6 inches below the line. This causes all kinds of tangling problems. Clements has two eyes, usually porcelain or agate, at either end of a 4-inch bar through which the reel line is run. The weight is still 6 inches below the boom but is prevented from swinging about to the same extent, so the risk of tangle with the trace is greatly reduced. Clements is unsuitable with any form of trace intended to flow out in the tide.

Basic terminal rigs

Paternoster. The trace carries two or more hooks and is particularly suitable for bottom fishing in slack water. It can be tied from a single length of monofilament to produce an average length trace of 3 ft with stand-off legs to carry the hooks.

To make one, form a loop in the line, pass the short loose end through the loop and around again twelve times, pick up centre of loop between thumb and forefinger and pass it back through the centre of the twists. Then pull gently on both sides until the knot is tight. The size of the starting loop dictates the size of the finished leg. If a double snood is required, as used in heavy-duty fishing, it is left as it is. For a single snood cut half of it away. The process is repeated along the length of the paternoster at 15-inch intervals.

A conventional paternoster is fished with the weight at the bottom but a variation is to place it on the reel line above the

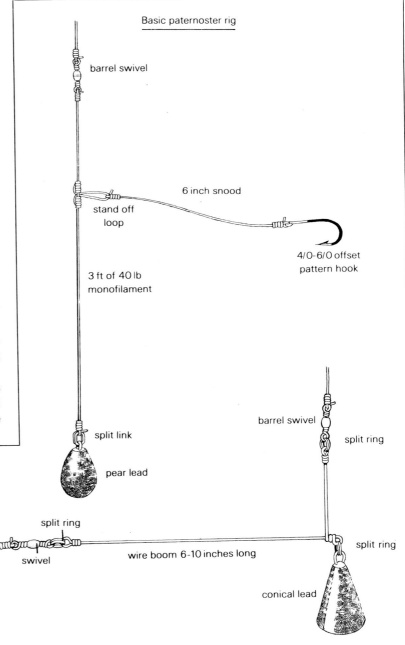

Basic paternoster rig

barrel swivel

6 inch snood

stand off loop

4/0-6/0 offset pattern hook

3 ft of 40 lb monofilament

split link

pear lead

barrel swivel

split ring

split ring

wire boom 6-10 inches long

conical lead

Flying collar rig

15-20 ft trace.

split ring

swivel

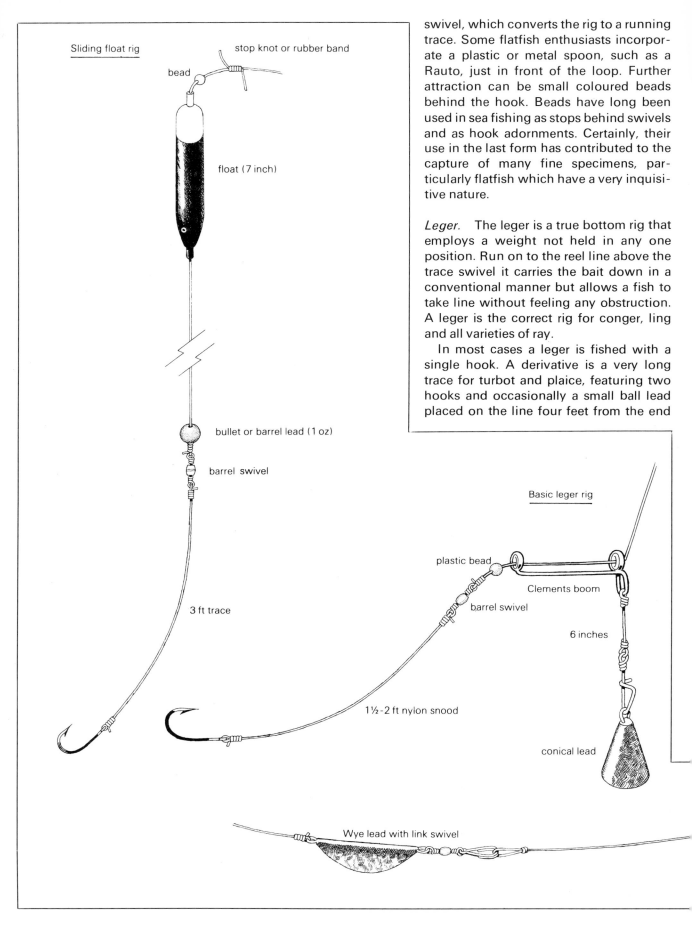

Sliding float rig

stop knot or rubber band

bead

float (7 inch)

bullet or barrel lead (1 oz)

barrel swivel

3 ft trace

swivel, which converts the rig to a running trace. Some flatfish enthusiasts incorporate a plastic or metal spoon, such as a Rauto, just in front of the loop. Further attraction can be small coloured beads behind the hook. Beads have long been used in sea fishing as stops behind swivels and as hook adornments. Certainly, their use in the last form has contributed to the capture of many fine specimens, particularly flatfish which have a very inquisitive nature.

Leger. The leger is a true bottom rig that employs a weight not held in any one position. Run on to the reel line above the trace swivel it carries the bait down in a conventional manner but allows a fish to take line without feeling any obstruction. A leger is the correct rig for conger, ling and all varieties of ray.

In most cases a leger is fished with a single hook. A derivative is a very long trace for turbot and plaice, featuring two hooks and occasionally a small ball lead placed on the line four feet from the end

Basic leger rig

plastic bead

Clements boom

barrel swivel

6 inches

1½-2 ft nylon snood

conical lead

Wye lead with link swivel

hook to assist in keeping the bait down as it passes over high banks of sand.

When heavy species with powerful mouths are being sought it is customary to use heavy commercial monofilament or strong wire for traces. Cable laid wire is sold by yacht and ships' chandlers.

Sliding float rig. Although principally used by shore anglers fishing from rocks and piers, what is termed the sliding float can be used to great advantage by the small-boat fisherman. It allows a bait to be fished at almost any depth and is particularly suitable for working across ground that would be too dangerous for the boat to approach.

This is how the rig is made up. A small bead is run on to the reel line, followed by a float with a hole through the middle (floats with eyes on the side are not suitable). Next comes a ball weight — 1 oz is sufficient for the average 7-inch sea float. A swivel is then tied to the line which traps all the items mentioned. To this is tied a 3 ft trace and hook. A rubber band is clove-hitched to the reel line above the bead. It is tight enough to remain in the desired position but can be slid under pressure to any point on the line. The distance between the rubber band and the swivel determines how deep the bait will be, e.g. placed 6 ft from it the bait will be nearly 10 ft below the surface.

Distance from swivel	6 ft
Length of trace	3 ft
Float, swivel, ball lead	9 ins
Total	9 ft 9 ins

The smaller the rubber stop the more easily it will pass through the rod rings, so surplus ends of rubber are cut away once the hitch has been tied.

Trolling rig. Working a natural or artificial bait behind a slow-moving boat is a long-established method of catching bass, pollack, coalfish and mackerel, usually over rough ground, with the bait allowed to work just above the bottom. At certain times, often just after first light and at dusk, the fish will rise high in the water to feed. Seabirds wheeling and diving are a clear indication that predators are chasing small fry which escape on the surface — out of the frying pan into the fire!

The trolling rig is a curved Jardine lead fastened behind a swivel 20 or more feet from the hook. Size depends on the speed of the boat (two to three knots is ideal) and the depth at which you want the bait. The bait or lure must work at least 100 yards astern to place it outside propeller interference. Once the lead reaches the rod tip, hooked fish are carefully drawn in the rest of the way hand over hand. Hooked fish are usually on the surface in the final seconds of the fight and do not put pressure on the trace, so there is normally no danger to bare hands.

Groundbaiting

The benefit of groundbaiting in shallow and medium depth water is often ignored by boat fishermen but simply throwing in chopped pieces of mackerel into water more than ten feet deep where there is a run of tide has no chance of drawing fish to the vicinity of the hook baits. The particles will be swept far beyond the area in a matter of a minute. The trick is to fill a sack or net onion bag with mashed-up fish laced with pilchard oil. Tie the bag to the anchor rope, just above the chain. The pieces of flesh and oil will now drift back where they will do the most good. Groundbaiting is never used in deep-water wreck fishing.

Shark fishing

The popularity of shark fishing grows by the year but, unfortunately, the tens of thousands of 'blues' caught in the last 20 years is now having an effect and fishing is not what it was.

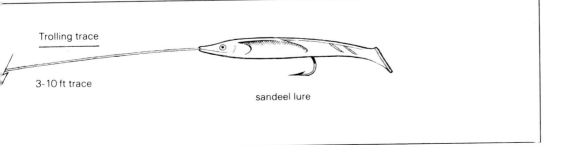

Trolling trace

3-10 ft trace

sandeel lure

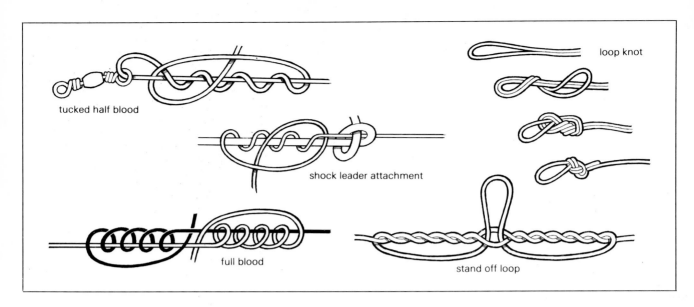

tucked half blood

shock leader attachment

full blood

loop knot

stand off loop

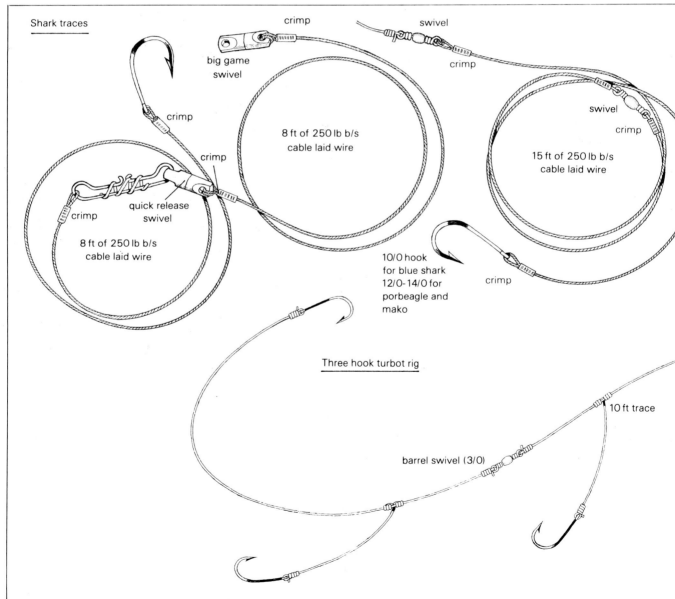

Shark traces

crimp

swivel

big game
swivel

crimp

crimp

crimp

8 ft of 250 lb b/s
cable laid wire

swivel

crimp

15 ft of 250 lb b/s
cable laid wire

quick release
swivel

crimp

8 ft of 250 lb b/s
cable laid wire

10/0 hook
for blue shark
12/0-14/0 for
porbeagle and
mako

crimp

Three hook turbot rig

10 ft trace

barrel swivel (3/0)

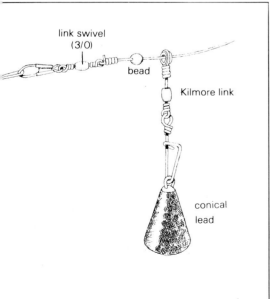

link swivel
(3/0)

bead

Kilmore link

conical
lead

Cornwall is the centre of Britain's shark fishing and fleets of boats make the 20 mile run out to the grounds daily from several ports, notably Looe, where it all began in the early 1950s.

The blue shark arrives in the lower English Channel in June and if the weather remains mild stays until quite late in the year. They have been caught in November, but that is extreme. Most weigh around 50 lb, but there is always the chance of a fish twice as big, in the early part of the season. If reasonably light tackle is used 'blues' give a good account of themselves.

Another shark, common to Cornish waters is the porbeagle, which is considerably heavier and harder fighting. The largest are found over reefs close inshore off the vaulting cliffs of the north Cornish coast. Giants, to the world record weight of 465 lb, have been taken near Crackington Haven and Hartland Point but fish

This big 9/0 multiplier reel is used for big game fishing, especially for sharks, as the large rod clamps securing the reel to the rod give evidence.

Opposite top Every angler needs to know a few simple knots. Here are some of the more basic knots for tying on hooks, swivels or lengths of line.

much bigger have been lost after protracted battles.

Ports specialising in porbeagle shark fishing include Padstow, Newquay and Appledore. Many trips begin just after dawn so you need to be an early riser.

Two other species, the man-eating mako and thresher also frequent Cornish waters but are rare in comparison with 'blues' and porbeagles. If you hook a mako it will be a big one.

Whatever the species, shark fishing should be done from a drifting boat with three baits out at different levels, usually set at 30, 60 and 100 ft. Baits, invariably mackerel, pilchard or herring, are suspended from balloon floats which can be seen even when a fair swell is running. Mackerel are obtained easily as hundreds are drawn to the boat by the 'rubby dubby' — a nauseous mixture of mashed fish and blood used to create a 'lane' to attract the shark.

A long trace is essential as sharks, especially porbeagles, have a habit of rolling it around their bodies. It is made up from 100-200 lb breaking strain cable laid wire, depending on which species are sought. When one of the baits is taken the others should be wound in as quickly as possible to avoid a tangle. No attempt is made to strike a shark until it has time to turn and swallow the bait. When the fish begins its second run the clutch on the reel is tightened up and the hook driven home firmly with a series of positive sweeps.

Correct and balanced tackle are key factors in successful boat fishing. Here are the combinations of rod, reel and line for each category, together with techniques for catching the popular species.

HARBOUR AND TIDAL RIVER FISHING

Two-handed 8-10 ft hollowglass
   spinning rod.
Small multiplier or skirted-spool reel.
Hook sizes 1, 1/0, 2/0.

Bottom fishing:
Single hook leger.
Monofilament line 10-15 lb b/s.
Plaice, dabs, flounders.

Float fishing:
Sliding or fixed float.
8 ft hollowglass rod.
Skirted or fixed-spool reel.

Hook sizes 1, 1/0, 2/0.
Mullet. 4-6 lb b/s.

Baited spoon fishing:
8-10 ft spinning rod, skirted-spool or
   small multiplier.
Spoons — plastic or thin metal — best
   colour varies from area to area.
   Experiment with different colours.
Hook sizes 1, 1/0.
Flounders, plaice, dabs, bass.
10-12 lb b/s.

Note — Very large conger live in harbours
   and tidal rivers.
Rod, 30 lb class 6½-7½ ft.
4/0 multiplier.
Hook sizes 8/0-10/0.
Wire trace or trace made up from tough
   commercial monofilament 30-40 lb b/s.

ESTUARY AND INSHORE BOAT FISHING

Two-handed hollowglass spinning rod.
12-15 lb test boat rod.
Small multiplier.
Fixed-spool reels are unsuitable except
   when working a float or drift-lining in a
   tide race for pollack, coalfish, bass,
   mackerel, garfish with 10-12 lb
   monofilament.

Bottom fishing:
Single hook leger.
Plaice, dabs, flounders, bream. 10-15 lb
   b/s.
Bass, wrasse, dogfish, cod, haddock,
   whiting, pouting. 12-18 lb b/s.
Turbot, thornback and small-eyed ray.
   18-24 lb b/s.

Note — If a multiple-hook paternoster is
   used for shoal fish, such as haddock,
   whiting and pouting, the strength of
   reel line should be 20 lb.
Hook sizes 1/0 — 4/0.
30 lb class rod.
4/0 multiplier.

Conger — 30-40 lb b/s line.
Wire trace, 18 inch (or commercial
   'mono').

DEEP WATER — REEF AND OPEN GROUND FISHING

This category deals with much larger fish so the weight of tackle is stepped up accordingly. Experts still employ a two-handed 10 ft spinning rod and small multiplier loaded with 12-15 lb line for free-swimming species, including pollack and coalfish, using the 'flying collar' method, but it is specialist fishing. A 12 lb class boat rod also fits this category.

Conventional flying collar fishing:
12, 15, 20 lb rod.
4/0 multiplier.
18-24 lb main line with 15-18 lb trace.
Hook sizes 3/0-4/0.
Pollack, coalfish.
15, 20, 30 lb test boat rod.
4/0 multiplier.
Hook sizes 4/0-6/0.
Single hook leger/multiple hook paternoster — black and red bream, whiting, dogfish, haddock, plaice, pouting. 18-24 lb b/s monofilament.
Single hook leger — ling, cod, turbot. 20-30 lb b/s.
Driftline — Tope. 20-36 lb b/s.

30 lb class rod.
3/0 multiplier.
Hook sizes 8/0-10/0.
Conger. 30-40 lb b/s.

50 lb class rod.
6/0 multiplier.
Hook sizes 12/0 forged eye.
Common skate. 50-60 lb b/s.

Large Jigger. 10/0-12/0 brazed eye treble hook.
Halibut.

WRECK FISHING

The biggest specimens of just about every species common to the waters of the British Isles are found on wrecks.

20, 30 lb class rod.
4/0 multiplier.
Hook sizes 2/0-4/0.
Black and red bream, pollack, coalfish, cod. 20-30 lb b/s.

30, 50 lb class rod.
4/0, 6/0 multiplier.
Hook sizes 10/0-12/0.
Conger, ling. 30-50 lb b/s.

Note — A specialist method of winter wreck fishing requiring much heavier tackle is described in the chapter on boat fishing techniques.

SHARK FISHING

20, 30 lb class rod.
4/0 multiplier.
Hook sizes 10/0-12/0.
Wire trace, minimum length 12 ft.
Blue shark. 20-40 lb b/s.

30, 50 lb rod.
6/0 multiplier.
Hook size 12/0.
Wire trace, minimum length 12 ft.
Porbeagle, thresher. 30-50 lb b/s.

50, 80 lb class rod.
9/0 multiplier.
Hook sizes 12/0-14/0.
Wire trace, minimum length 18 ft.
Mako. 80 lb b/s.

Shorefishing techniques

Fish are by no means evenly distributed and may only be present in fair numbers at certain times of the tide or year. If you live reasonably near the sea the local tackle shop will tell you what is being caught and where. Another good source of accurate, up-to-date information is the weekly coastal reports in *Angler's Mail* which covers virtually the whole of our coastline.

Having decided where you are going, the next step is to find out at what stage of the tide you should be there to have the best chance of catching fish. As a rule of thumb, the incoming flood tide fishes better than the outgoing ebb, though your

local tackle dealer is, once again, the best man to advise on this score. You can confirm the times of high and low water from a tide table booklet or by telephoning the nearest Coastguard station. High tide varies from area to area by as much as six hours, so it is important to calculate local differences based on the times given in most tide tables for high water at London Bridge. Remember that high tide time also advances each day by between 20 and 45 minutes. Your tackle dealer will probably be able to sell you a booklet listing tide times for the nearest major shipping port covering the whole of a year.

It is important when fishing on a crowded beach to keep a safe distance from your neighbour to avoid tangling lines. Note the use of spades as makeshift rod rests.

If you are fishing a shore mark for the first time and cannot obtain definite advice on the best stage of the tide to fish, try the last three hours of the flood up to high water and for an hour and a half afterwards. Most beaches produce fish from May to Christmas after which there is generally a marked lull in sport. Once again your local tackle shop or the *Angler's Mail* reports will confirm the local trends.

Weather greatly affects shorefishing. In very rough conditions it is virtually impossible to fish effectively. While the fish may be there, it is tough casting tackle into strong winds and even harder to keep it on the bottom. Rough water picks up the end tackle and hurls it all over the place. It is usually deposited on the tideline some distance down from you along with seaweed and driftwood. Weed is another menace as great banks of it sometimes appear in rough seas, hanging on the line like washing and making fishing more trouble than it is worth.

At the other extreme, flat calm conditions are not always ideal, particularly in daylight. When the sea is calm for a long period it becomes clear and fish are reluctant to expose themselves in daylight. So it's often a case of evening and night fishing in still conditions.

But good fishing weather is never far away. The ideal conditions are a bit of surf, movement and colour in the water. This stirs up the bottom, dislodging scraps of food and also gives colour to the water which is cover for the naturally cautious fish.

Having arrived at the fishing mark the next step is to tackle up as described earlier and for bait there is no better general-purpose offering than lugworm. Of all the shop-bought baits they are the most widely available and there are few commonly-caught shore fish that will not take lugworm readily. When baiting up, hold the hook firmly between finger and thumb at the eye. Push the point through the head of the worm then thread the hook through its middle, completely covering the bend and shank. Do not worry if the worm bursts or bits of juice flow from it, for this escaping juice is attractive to fish. With a big lugworm you will probably find it necessary to thread the bait past the hook eye and partly up the line before the point protrudes. It is always preferable to load the hook with too much bait rather than too little. Good

Fishing for whiting on the East Anglian coast, this beach caster watches for the tell-tale sharp raps on the rod tip which are the trademark of the whiting's bold bite.

anglers argue that with greedy fish like cod, it is impossible to cram too many worms on the hook and up the line. As a rule of thumb, smaller species demand only enough bait to fill the hook. But with larger species like cod, fill the hook and add half as much again.

Finding the most productive spot on a beach requires a great deal of experience. It involves looking at the beach and figuring out where the fish will swim once it has been covered by the tide. Look for gullies and other likely food holding points and remember the basic rules of fish movement are governed by the hunt for food and fear of being seen. If you can find an area of the beach where these two basic items come together you are on the way to finding the best spot.

Shore crabs are so prolific around all the shores of Britain in spring, summer and autumn that they will pick baited hooks clean in less than 15 minutes, so you cannot leave a bait out indefinitely waiting for a fish to come along. Clearly, if your bait has been eaten away you will have to shorten the length of time it is in the water. If the bait comes back more or less intact, which is usually the case in the winter months when the crabs have moved out, then you can extend the length of time the bait is left.

There is no need to remove all the bait and replace it with fresh every time you cast out. In normal fishing this is wasteful and unnecessary. If you are using small worms, simply push another one on to the hook, giving a fresh smell and taste to the bait.

When tackling up, the first decision is to select a suitable sinker. There are two basic patterns — the wire-grip models which anchor on the seabed and those without wires which have an aerodynamic shape for smooth casting. The latter are used where there is little tidal flow or where there are a lot of rocks. On rocky ground anchor sinkers almost inevitably become firmly snagged. A plain sinker does not trap so easily.

You are likely to have a choice of 4, 5 or 6 oz sinkers but it is advisable to always use a 5 oz weight. You will find it easier to cast consistently when you use the same weight every time. Besides, the advantages gained from varying the weight are minimal.

After casting out the tide immediately carries the line downtide and instead of pointing straight out in the direction you have cast, the line takes up an angle of 45° away from you. This is caused by strong tidal flow pushing the tackle downtide before the wires have dug into the bottom. To avoid this problem, walk up the beach parallel with the tideline for about 20 yards and then cast normally. The line will have been swept away at an angle again before the wires have dug in, but then you walk back to your fishing position to counteract that initial sweep and take up the angle, so that the line is now in a straight line out from your fishing position. Alternatively, cast out at a 45° angle to your position, so that by the time the wires have dug in the tackle is more or less in front of you.

Make sure there is plenty of room between you and the next angler to avoid tackle tangles. If possible, allow 15 yards between yourself and the next angler so that a wayward cast does not result in crossed lines. Even if you are casting straight out, 15 yards is a good average courtesy distance between you and the next angler.

Having cast out, set up the monopod or tripod and position the rod so that it rests about halfway up the rod. If there is a lot of tide pull or wind which causes the rod top to sway about wildly, slide the rod further down the rest so that just a couple of feet protrude beyond the rest. This will reduce the amount of tip movement.

The rod tip will bend and straighten in a fairly predictable and steady rhythm, caused by the tide, wind and breakers. But if it jerks erratically this is the sign that a fish has picked up the bait and is trying to make off with it or tear it loose from the hook. To set the hook in the fish's mouth, grasp the rod with both hands in a similar position to which you would hold the butt during casting and sweep the rod back away from the sea. You can improve this even further by stepping or running backwards for a couple of feet which will take up any slack line. Do not step or run backwards on rocky ground and be careful at night or else you may fall.

A bite is also signalled if the line goes very slack. This is because the fish has picked up the bait and run inshore with all the tackle. When this happens take up the slack as fast as possible before attempting to set the hook. On sand or shingle, run backwards until you feel the tackle go tight. But on rocks reel in the slack line as fast as possible before striking.

When the fish is hooked do not be in too much of a hurry. Reeling in too fast can often tear the hook from the fish's mouth, particularly if it is not set firmly. If the fish is small you can reel in steadily without too much trouble. But with bigger fish it will be necessary to 'pump' the catch ashore. It works like this. Point the rod in the direction of the line and tighten up. Stop reeling and steadily lift the rod, which will bring in several yards of line. Stop the lift when the rod reaches vertical and then start to reel in while at the same time lowering the rod. As the rod lowers, it releases the tension on the tackle and would give slack line but for the fact you are taking up this slack line on the reel. When the rod has reached horizontal the procedure begins all over again. 'Pumping' should be done steadily and smoothly and with as few pauses in between strokes of the rod as possible.

When the fish is almost at the water's edge, time the last few 'pumps' so that you draw the fish in as a wave is surging forward. This will give you additional lift and deposit the fish high and dry on the beach. If you try to pull the fish through the surf when a wave is rushing back, the force of this backwash could tear the fish from the hook just as you are about to beach it.

Before leaving this subject it would be useful also to describe two methods of holding the rod and reel during reeling in. The first is to trap the rod butt between closed legs so that the reel is just above waist height. Grip the rod firmly just above the reel with one hand and wind in the line with the other. Which hand does which job depends on the reel and whether you are left- or right-handed. If you are using a multiplier, of which there are extremely few left-hand wind models, then the left hand will always grip the rod and the right the reel handle. The multiplier is then on top of the rod, the correct position for winding in. The level of the line on the multiplier must always be kept flat. This is achieved by pinching the line with the finger and thumb of the left hand and guiding it evenly to and fro across the spool. This sounds cumbersome but is an easy practice to master.

If preferred, the rod butt can be tucked under the left armpit, trapping the butt about a foot below the reel. Then use the right hand to reel in as previously described. The level of line is kept steady by the finger and thumb of the free left hand, which holds and supports the rod above the reel.

Multiplier over-runs are almost certainly caused by a jerky cast which sets the reel spool spinning so fast that more line is coming off the reel than the weight can take away. A useful dodge is to reduce the amount of line on your reel. Try casting with only half a reel-full. Less line comes off the reel per revolution so the weight can take it away without snarling up. This is also a useful tip when casting into a strong wind.

If your tackle trundles downtide and swings close inshore almost before your rod is in the rest, use one of the wired anchoring sinkers.

Having got your fish on there is nothing more frustrating than to find as you wind in that the tackle has become stuck on some seabed obstruction such as a clump of weed or rock. To help avoid this in the first place, reel in, as quickly as you can. This will force the tackle to plane up from the bottom and so miss the seabed obstructions.

Should you get snagged up while a fish is on, there are three things you can do. Try pulling hard to see if the tackle will come free of its own accord, but do not at this stage pull hard enough to snap the line. If that does not work try releasing the spool and allow the line to go very slack. This will allow the fish to swim back out and it sometimes happens that in doing so it will release the tackle from the snag.

Alternatively, slack off again, and walk 100 yards up the beach and tighten up and pull. The pressure applied at a different angle may release the tackle. Do it in both directions. If none of these ideas work you have no other choice than to just apply direct pressure to the line to see what gives first — the snag or the line.

If you keep getting bites but never seem to hook a fish, have a cast without any bait on. Daft as that sounds, it could well be that your lack of experience is interpreting the movement of the rod through wind and wave action as that caused by a fish. If you have no bait on and the rod is still behaving in the same manner you know the problem!

If no fish are forthcoming after a few casts, and you feel they should be about, try varying the distance you cast. Fish often come close in and a long cast could be over-reaching them. Alternatively, move further down the beach for 100 yards or so and see if a different location brings you better luck. It often happens that fish are staying put in one spot and it might be closer to you than you think.

Often when you catch a fish the hook is lodged just inside the mouth and you can take hold of the hook and waggle it out. Sometimes, however, the hook will be deep inside the throat and getting it out can be a problem. If you intend to keep the fish for eating and it is deeply hooked, knock it on the head while still attached to kill it. Then break open the gill covers and you will be able to dislodge the hook from inside the mouth.

Night fishing is often more productive than daylight fishing, and while many aspects of shorefishing are the same no

A good haul of whiting caught on a night fishing expedition.

matter whether day or night, there are a few extra things to remember in night fishing.

Since there is no natural light, you have to carry your own artificial light and the two most popular sources are a paraffin pressure lamp and a torch. A torch is the cheapest but the paraffin pressure lamp is the brightest and most useful.

Some anglers prefer a small, battery-powered headlight that is strapped round the forehead or you could tie a loop of ribbon around a bicycle lamp and hang it from your neck. Whatever your light source it will have to be directed at the rod tip so that you can see the movement of the tip and recognise a bite. To assist in seeing the rod tip in the dark, wrap some white or reflective tape round the top six inches of the rod or paint it white.

Another problem you will encounter is that it is a darned sight colder at night, so increase the amount of warm clothing you are wearing and take a flask. Even in summer night fishing can be chilly work.

After the day's fishing is finished and you have some fish you wish to prepare for eating, it is wise to gut the fish. Leaving the guts inside many sea fish is to ask for a rapid decomposition of the flesh, along with an unpalatable tainting. Gut a fish by inserting a sharp, pointed knife up the vent and cutting right up the belly to the head. Pull the insides out, throw them into the sea and wash the fish in the surf.

Piers. These are popular places to begin shorefishing as those who cannot cast very far can reach deep water with a modest cast. There is nothing difficult about fishing from piers and no specialist tackle is needed. You may well be able to find out the nature of the seabed you are fishing over by looking at the beach when the tide has gone out, for many piers are left dry at low tide.

Rocks. These can be very productive but are also very dangerous, particularly at night and when the sea is rough. Rocks often fish well because they extend into the sea and provide a lot of cover for small fish, shellfish, crabs and the like. The drawback is that you may lose tackle on the rocks when you get fastened up . . . but you cannot have it all ways. If your tackle losses start mounting, use stronger line or improvised sinkers such as an old spark plug or big nuts and bolts. You may even have to fish line as heavy as 35 lb to avoid losing your tackle every time you get fastened up.

Harbours. Fishing from harbour walls is rather like pier fishing. Frequently you can catch fish close in and there is no need for a long cast. Harbours usually tend to fish in the warmer months when fish such as mackerel, flatties, pollack and coalfish, or eels are about. If there is a reasonable depth of water you can try fishing right down the side of the wall. You could also try float fishing with a largish freshwater float that will allow you to suspend a bait in midwater.

Sandy beaches. These shores often demand a good, long cast to reach deeper water so they are the hardest type of mark for the newcomer. It is far better to use just one bait — for maximum streamlining. These beaches usually fish best at high water.

Estuaries. Another place where long casting may not be needed as the estuary could have deepish water fairly close in. The great problem is the increased tidal flow as the current forces up-river. Anchor leads are essential but one advantage is that estuaries frequently produce fish through all stages of the tide.

Spinning. A very pleasant method of shorefishing as it involves constant action. Spinning is casting out a weighted lure that is meant to resemble a small food fish and it is retrieved through the water as soon as it has been cast out. These lures, called spinners or flies, often do not look like a fish to the human eye, but as they are brought through the water they flash and fool fish. Spinning is usually done in the warmer months with light tackle and is successful only for a limited number of species. It is something to watch out for when you are fishing in summer and if you see someone doing it successfully in an area where you regularly fish then you may wish to buy a spinning tackle rig and take it up. Fish that respond to spinners and flies are mackerel, pollack, coalfish and bass.

Piers are ideal for those who do not have specialist tackle and cannot cast very far. On a good day there are always plenty of other anglers about, as this photograph shows, who would be willing to give advice on baits and tackle.

At high tide these harbour walls are packed with young anglers who can fish for a wide variety of species in comfort and safety.

Species	Fishing Venues	Recommended Rig and Bait
Bass	Prefer warmish water and not common in the northern half of the country and Scotland. Otherwise found over all types of ground and in estuaries.	A large hook with a large bait such as peeler crab or a big worm bait. No need to cast a long way as they come close in. Single hook rig preferred.
Cod	All types from smooth sand to rocky edges, piers and estuaries. Found all round Britain except for the south-west where few are caught from the shore.	Where distance casting is needed, a single hook though two hooks can be used when pier fishing. Worm is the most popular bait but peeler crab, and shellfish can also be used.
Dabs and Plaice	Smooth, sandy ground; mud or fine shingle, definitely not rocky ground. Found all round Britain where the ground is suitable.	Two hooks or even three if the fish are plentiful. Small hooks, size 2 or 4, are best for the small-mouthed species, and worm is the top bait.
Dogfish	Clear, warmish water; mainly a summer species, found all round Britain on both smooth and rocky ground.	Single-hook rig with fish strip or worm; will also take crab.
Flounders	Universally distributed where the ground is clear of rocks. Particularly like mud and brackish water in estuaries.	Similar tackle to dabs and plaice but the addition of a bright bead or small spoon just above the bait can often increase catches. Peeler crab is a deadly bait, otherwise worms.
Mackerel	At times can be found all round Britain, but mostly in high summer and early autumn and mostly where the water is warmish and clear.	For sport, a small spinner on a light rod is great fun. A light rod with a small piece of mackerel fished either on the bottom or on a freshwater float.
Pollack and Coalfish	Clear water and often rocky ground, though occasionally found over sand. Located all round Britain.	Spinning with spoons or Toby lures in the evening off rock edges. Bait fishing with a single-hook rig, worm bait or a piece of fish.
Whiting	All types of ground, from rocky edges to smooth sand but not in brackish estuaries. Not common in the south-west as they prefer colder water.	A single-hook rig where distance casting is needed but if the whiting are coming close in a two-hook rig can be used with 1/0 or 2/0 hooks. Worms or a piece of mackerel best baits.
Wrasse	Clear, warm water and rocks a must as wrasse live in and around rocks. In summer can be found all round Britain where conditions are right.	A single-hook rig just lobbed off a rock edge into a pool where the wrasse will be lying. Worm or shellfish favourite bait. Crabs are particularly deadly.

Boat fishing techniques

Charter boat fishing

There are many ports around the coast of Britain where charter boats are available for hire, mostly on a day basis. At a few places, principally holiday towns such as Newquay in Cornwall, there are skippers who operate morning, afternoon or evening trips. These can be an advantage if the family has to be considered but spectacular results cannot be expected as due to the time factor, the actual fishing will be within a few miles of land. Evening trips are usually between 7.30 and 10.30 pm in the summer months and can be rewarding if a skipper offers a specific type of fishing — for example, conger, pollack or whiting. This sort of outing is quite different from the two-hour mackerel trip with feathers which is fun for a complete beginner but hardly sea fishing in its true sense.

Charter boat fishing varies enormously with the range of operations and quality usually dictated by the geography of the area. A trip from an East Coast port, such as Lowestoft, will be within six miles of land in water no more than 15 fathoms deep. In all probability, the boat will be capable of carrying only a maximum of six anglers and will not have much in electronic equipment beyond a radio and an echo-sounder.

At leading West Country fishing ports the great majority of craft are over 32 ft in length, licensed to operate within a radius of 50 miles and equipped with every conceivable electronic aid, such as a Decca Navigator, sophisticated echo-sounder and fish finder, VHF and ship-to-shore radio, radar and, in some cases, a magnetometer which records the presence of iron lying on the seabed, an invaluable aid to locating unfished wrecks.

Before a boat is awarded the licence to operate, it is subjected to a detailed survey by a qualified boatmaster usually appointed by a local authority. Life-saving equipment is of the greatest importance and there must be enough inflatable rafts for everyone aboard. It is not permissible to have one very large raft, a minimum of two is the rule. If one proves faulty the other can support people in the water until help arrives. Skippers are put through a stiff test on seamanship, navigation and general knowledge of the area in which they are to work.

All licensed craft must display a notice stating the number of passengers and crew allowed, the position of the life-saving equipment and flares, and what to do in an emergency. Many also list information on how to operate the radio, should the skipper meet with an accident.

This all adds up to a feeling of great security, which is no mean thing when 40 miles from port in a waste of sea that is a cruel enemy.

It is asking for trouble to sail in a non-licensed boat with a 'cowboy' skipper at a very cheap price. These persons are gradually being weeded out of the angling business but there will always be a few around.

The perfect boat in which to spend a long day afloat must be somewhere in the future. At present the nearest to it is a craft of not less than 30 ft in length, with a 12 ft beam. It must have a main and a wing engine capable of returning it to port at a steady five knots and have a wheel-house, or a shelter behind it, capable of holding all the people aboard.

Wreck fishing craft, which operate over the greatest distances, must have facilities for heating food and drinks and seating for at least half the complement. A flush toilet in a cubicle is essential.

The etiquette of charter boat fishing

Above A group of anglers have chartered a boat for the day, one of the many craft available all round our coast.

Left Typical layout of electronics on a wreck boat. They include a Decca Navigator, echo-sounder and ship-to-shore radio.

demands that the skipper has the very considerable responsibility of your safety. Never question any order he gives and always react to it quickly. If he decides to head for home somewhat earlier than expected, the decision will probably have been based on a changing weather pattern. Many skippers long on experience, often from a lifetime at sea, have an uncanny instinct and can literally smell a front moving in.

Before considering perhaps 12 hours at sea on a wreck fishing expedition, the possibility of sea sickness must be taken into account. If there is a tendency to this it is best to stick to 8.30 am to 5.30 pm trips, the average duration of a reef or open ground charter. If you feel ill return to port is then a known time but in wreck fishing it is usually 'over the horizon' without a scheduled return time.

No reef skipper with a full complement out for a day's sport is likely to return simply because one person is constantly sick. In top-class wrecking, where all but two fish are retained by the skipper, abandoning the session before time would only be done as a very last resort. Various seasick remedies are available but it would be foolish to rely totally on them without first taking a few less demanding trips.

Clothing is of vital importance in every aspect of boat fishing. Temperatures are very different once outside the shelter of land. A breeze coming off the sea can be positively chilling and without adequate protection the body cools rapidly. Cold is a prime inducer of seasickness. By far the best protection is obtained from a one-piece waterproof suit with a hood that can be drawn tight to the face with a cord. Some are classed as flotation suits and will keep a person afloat for a long period if an accident occurs. In normal use they keep out the wind and rain and maintain body temperature. Underneath, trousers and a good quality wool sweater over a T-shirt are best. Cold feet make for a miserable day, so wear thick socks, preferably those made for fishermen, and a decent pair of short rubber boots with non-slip soles. Those made for yachtsmen fit the bill perfectly. Thigh boots have no place in boat fishing and should be avoided like the plague. A woolly hat and a pair of gloves complete the outfit.

Unless it is a perfect summer day with no wind and a sea like a mill pond, the suit should be put on before leaving harbour. It is all too easy for a wave to come over the side unexpectedly and give one a soaking to the skin.

Enough good food and drink for roughly twice the expected duration of the trip is not a bad precaution. If a breakdown occurs it can be waited out well fed, warm and dry.

A boat kit should contain a small first-aid box holding various size plasters, bandages, iodine and a square of clean white linen. Charter boats have a first-aid kit as part of required equipment but it is best to be self-supporting wherever possible.

Anglers are allowed to take only two fish at the conclusion of a charter no matter how many have been caught. Space prevents full discussion on the reasons for this rule but it exists in top-flight wreck fishing, particularly at ports in the South West of England. Fishing with a skipper who keeps part of the catch for sale has its advantages. He has one aim in life — to see his clients catch big specimens and plenty of them. So he makes sure they are placed over a hotspot. The clients are doing what they set out to do — catch fish. At the end of the outing they can each pick two of the best, which could mean 50 lb of prime ling fillets.

Not for one moment is it suggested that skippers who do not operate the fish rule do not try their best to locate a good mark. Many believe the actual charter fee for the boat, which is now around £100 and rising, is sufficient. Which type of charter to take is for the individual to decide. What is important is to ascertain the terms of contract when the booking is made. Unfortunately, many anglers do not do this, which results in an unpleasant argument after the boat has docked with a deck full of fish. If clients wish to keep all they catch they should book on a boat where there is no fish limit. Without exception, skippers who operate reef or open-ground fishing trips do not impose any kind of restriction.

Fishing positions on the boat are for the party to decide. The fairest way is to have a draw in which the number drawn relates to a given place in the boat for the entire day. Alternatively, a second draw midway through the trip can be held but this means a complete upheaval of gear and bodies, and is not recommended.

If the anglers are known to each other the question of fishing places will be resolved as a matter of course. With parties of individuals, the skipper should assume responsibility for organising the lottery. Fishing places in the boat can be all-important. Stern places are most prized, as these avoid the problem of keeping out of the way of others plus the advantage of fishing squarely to the tide. A conger in the 60 lb class can be pumped more easily with the rod bending straight in front rather than from a side angle. If a harness is used the full weight of the fish can be transferred to the shoulders while the arms take a rest. The rod butt, of course, rests in the cup of a belly pad. No matter which position is drawn, if a very large fish is hooked, the angler should be allowed to move to a stern position. Once the giant is safely secured, he then returns to his original fishing place.

Twelve anglers working in a confined space obviously demands a high level of co-operation if half the day is not to be wasted untangling reel lines and terminal tackle. Assuming six men are fishing each side of the boat, those in the bow end should use heavier weights than those nearer the stern. The effect is to keep the terminal rigs apart when they are on the bottom. Different length rods are the complete answer to the problem with the anglers fishing from the bow having the longest rods which allow a rig to work a foot or so outside the zone of the bottom being worked by the next man down.

Many boat fishing specialists take as many as six rods on a trip, all of different lengths and class. Some go to the trouble of having their rods custom-built to suit certain species or tidal conditions and to cope with the eventuality of drawing an unfortunate forward fishing position. It is a fact that 12 men who consistently fish together can make huge catches with very few tangles. When they do occur, little time is wasted sorting it out. A knife solves the problem in seconds — a trifle heavy on monofilament and, perhaps expensive wire traces to forged eye hooks, but it is all in the interest of keeping the flow of fish coming up from the wreck.

Gone are the days when a skipper relied on his knowledge, a keen pair of eyes and binoculars to locate a mark far out at sea by lining up certain objects on the land. Haze often rendered the task hopeless and it was then a case of shifting around in the hope of bumping into fish or taking a chance and anchoring up. This often resulted in a great waste of time as there were frequent shifts.

Electronics have solved the problem and the modern skipper puts his faith in a sensitive echo-sounder, or better still, in a Decca Navigator, worked in conjunction with a graph-type sounder, to find a mark unerringly. Each wreck or reef, or even part of a reef, known to the skipper is given a set of co-ordinate numbers which he guards jealously. Shore stations continually send out signals which display as numbers on green, red and purple dials on the Decca console in the boat. These give a three-directional cross-bearing of the craft's position in relation to lane bands on a specially marked-up chart.

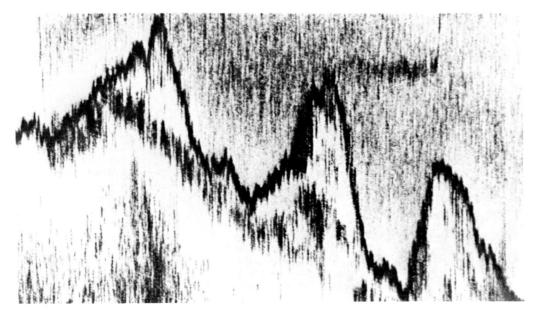

A graph-type echo-sounder shows the bottom configuration at a famous mark off the south coast of Devon. Ground of this type gives shelter to many species of fish, particularly ling, pollack and bream.

A coalfish is brought aboard by two well kitted-out anglers. Their bright waterproof suits are vital to their safety and warmth; even though it may be a sunny day a breeze coming off the sea can be very chilling.

Opposite top When chartering a boat for the day it is very important to decide the fishing positions before the trip starts; several anglers working in a confined space demands a high level of co-operation.

Opposite bottom Wreck fishing offers the angler the chance of catching the largest fish. Here a group of well organised anglers is making a superb catch of ling and conger.

The Decca is accurate to within 12 ft but a sounder is needed for correct positioning. The instrument sends a signal to the bottom through a transducer in the hull. The time it takes to return is measured electronically and depicted as a black image on special recording paper.

The very latest technology is a sounder that works in seven colours without the need of a paper image. It is only a matter of time before this equipment is fitted to a charter angling craft.

The most sophisticated sounders build up a picture of the bottom, what lies on it, shoals of fish and even large individual specimen fish.

All this equipment and a skipper's skill in interpreting the information it gives, leads anglers to incredible catches, particularly of conger, ling, pollack and coalfish which haunt wrecks in large numbers.

Wrecks

Victims of storms and two world wars litter the bottom of the sea around Britain's coastline and provide shelter for hoards of fish. Once they have taken up residence some species remain there for the rest of their lives. Conger generally hide in the bottom levels of wreckage. Some enter parts of a wreck through small holes when young fish and then grow so large they are eventually trapped inside. They feed on fish passing through and over a period of years reach enormous weights.

A wreck lying 32 fathoms deep off South Devon has a conger in a boiler. The conger is big enough to smash the British record but it can never leave its home.

Ling tend to move all over the wreckage but rarely rise higher than 40 ft. Pollack often swim well above the top part with the coalfish but there are no hard and fast rules for bream, although the biggest usually hug the bottom.

With few exceptions, wreck fishing gives anglers the chance of the largest fish but there is evidence that over-fishing and the consequent removal of vast numbers has created a generation gap in several species. Wrecks once alive with conger, ling and pollack are now virtually barren and skippers have to go as much as 40 miles from land to make catches in excess of 1000 lb.

In the early days double that weight could have been made by ten men in about five hours at wrecks only an hour's run from many West Country ports. Marks left alone for a few years build up reasonable stocks once again and thoughtful skippers with an eye to the future work them on a rotation system which pays off handsomely.

Wrecks lying in deep water where fast tides are common can be fished only during small neaps. Being a good way out from land weather also plays a role, so visits to them are irregular, which preserves, to some extent, their stock of fish. Good examples are wrecks in Start Bay and Lyme Bay off the Devon and Dorset coast where the tide positively spates and will buoy up 2 lb of lead.

In this situation it is impossible to get a bait on the bottom while the boat is at anchor. The run of water is judged by putting a dan-buoy over the wreck fastened to a 56 lb scale weight. The dan carries five or six plastic containers, which are often pulled right under when the tide is at its greatest flow, leaving just the flag as a marker. As it slackens the bottles gradually break surface. When only one is submerged the skipper goes to anchor and fishing can begin.

Tides

The movement of water has a great influence on fish behaviour. It would be unwise to make a sweeping statement that fish do not feed in slack water but it is close to the truth, particularly inshore. As slack water approaches most species become lethargic and remain in that state for the relatively short time between old and new tide. It is quite amazing how fish that have been feeding freely will stop together, as if a signal had been given. It happens too many times to be a coincidence. Even in deep water, especially on wrecks where there is a large head of fish, there is always a period when the sea seems devoid of life. This usually occurs in the last half-hour of the tide and continues for a similar time into the new.

The most productive fishing period at a wreck is generally from the middle of the first hour to the end of the third. Some wrecks fish well on a flood tide, others give best catches during the ebb. Which way the wreck is lying on the bottom also has a bearing. If the wreck is whole and on its side with the open part facing down channel, the greatest catches will be made during the up-channel run. Wrecks that are well broken, or sitting upright on the bottom, are marks for flood or ebb-tide fishing. When planning a deep-water fishing trip more than eight miles from the coast it should be remembered that high or low water will be approximately three hours later than times published in tide tables.

Tidal flow through an average tide of 6 hours 15 minutes is roughly one-twelfth in the first and sixth hours, two-twelfths in the second and fourth hours and three-twelfths in the third and fifth hours.

Uptide fishing

A long boat rod, which has a very flexible action is just right for what has become known as uptide fishing. When working flat, muddy or sandy ground the technique is to cast the terminal tackle as far uptide from the boat as possible and allow it to work back across the bottom with the current. This permits a great deal of ground to be covered although the boat is stationary on the anchor.

If the tide is very fast, a wired grip-lead between 4 and 8 oz will increase the actual time the bait is fishing. It is as well to remember that a tidal run of five knots, which is common in many places during the spring tide period, puts considerable pressure on the bellied line and end gear and will carry it at least 30 yards back towards the boat before it hits bottom, if the depth of water is more than 60 ft. The size of bait being used also has a big bearing on the speed of drift. The larger it is the faster the terminal tackle will move.

Casting a flowing trace of even 3 ft from a crowded charter boat is not without danger. For this reason many skippers do not allow uptide fishing. In any event the method can only be employed in reasonably calm conditions.

Drift fishing

A great deal of winter fishing is carried out by drifting over wrecks with the tide after dan-buoys have been dropped at both ends to mark accurately the hulk's position in relation to the tidal stream. The biggest pollack catches are made during spring tide periods, when the fish are stirred into frenzied feeding activity by the fast run of water. At this time they will strike at lures and natural baits with little regard to caution.

Big tides ensure swift and accurate drifts across the wreckage and it is possible to get in several dozen during a single tide of six hours.

Working on the drift with artificial lures is most successful when not more than six anglers fish at a time. The boat moves sideways down the length or across the hulk, so the lines stream out naturally from one side only. Fishing from the wrong side, with the lines going under the keel, is unpleasant and difficult. There are unnecessary tangles, hooked fish are frequently lost and, most important of all, valuable fishing time is wasted. It is also a fact that too many leads plummeting down to the wreck at the same time frighten the fish, which puts them off the feed.

Much of the winter fishing off Devon and Cornwall is with strong nylon paternosters, rigged with either two or three artificial eels on short snoods. The nylon must not be less than 50 lb breaking strain as it may have to cope with a couple of fish weighing well over 16 lb apiece at the same time. In this situation, pollack tend to 'run' in opposite directions after taking the lures, which puts a tremendous strain on the knots. If three artificials are being used, which is typical rod and line 'commercial' practice, the strength of the rig is stepped up to 80 lb breaking strain. Even this has been known to break under the weight of fish.

A completely different and more sporting approach is a single lure to a long trace worked from a wire boom, the 'flying collar' rig mentioned earlier, or the recently introduced plastic variety. This effectively prevents the trace from tangling with the reel line during its long journey through perhaps 40 fathoms of water to the bottom. After reaching the wreck or reef, the trace is steadily retrieved until the lure is taken, at which point the pollack will make its characteristic plunge for freedom. Line must be given under pressure from the slipping clutch or a break off is a certainty. A fish of 18 lb is quite capable of making five or more powerful dives as it is played to the surface from a deep wreck, as on the 'flying collar' rig it has more time to adjust to changing water pressure, its greatest enemy. A good run of tide is essential if the long trace is to work correctly.

Pirk fishing

Pirks are also effective for winter fishing sessions but a great deal of stamina is necessary to work a large one correctly for

long periods. Successful pirking has been developed to a fine art by charter boat skippers who stand high on the bows, well out of the way of their anglers, and hurl the lure as far as they can, letting it plunge unchecked to the bottom. It is then retrieved at speed with a high-geared multiplier, until a fish grabs it. Very large pollack and coalfish, and occasionally ling, feature in catches made by this method.

The effectiveness of large wreck pirks, which weigh up to 26 oz, can be enhanced by the addition of coloured plastic streamers and natural baits, such as a half-side of mackerel or a thin strip of squid.

Pirk fishing on open and rough ground

for cod is a favourite method in Scottish waters, particularly at the Gantocks, a renowned mark in the Clyde. The best months are January and February. But the days when numerous fish in the 40 to 45 lb class were caught are now some years in the past. Even so, cod in double-figures are still taken regularly. Much smaller pirks are used than in the wreck situation, the average weight being about 12 oz. The run of tide really dictates the size.

The correct rod should be about 7 ft long and have a fast taper with plenty of power in the butt. Unlike wreck fishing the lure is worked up and down so that it flutters. Many fish brought up on a pirk will be

Opposite A fine catch of conger and turbot from a wreck in the west of England.

A selection of pirks for deep sea fishing. These lures are effective, especially in winter, for pollack, coalfish and cod. However, they take a great deal of stamina to use correctly for long periods.

hooked in the side of the head or just in front of the dorsal fin as they usually make slashing sideways attacks.

Closely allied to pirks are various types of lures which are worked with a sink-and-draw action to attract a fish. Among them are highly coloured plastic squid mounted in threes on a nylon trace. Having no weight of their own it requires a lead of at least 10 oz, to take them down reasonably quickly to a good depth.

Halibut, the largest of all flatfish, are caught on very big jiggers up to 3 lb in weight, which are often baited with a flatfish. Worked in the deep water tide races off Caithness, Orkney and Shetland, these have accounted for fish of 200 lb. Halibut of this size tend to hunt alone but others are likely to be in the same area. Once hooked they come to the surface fairly quickly but after seeing daylight they begin a fight that can last an hour. A giant sounding at speed is said to be the most exciting experience in saltwater angling.

Terminal rigs

Simplicity is important in boat fishing. There is absolutely no need for complicated 'Christmas tree' rigs of wire booms, multiple swivels and the like, yet these are constantly seen in use.

Artificial eels imitate a swimming fish and much design work goes into achieving that objective, yet all too often they have strips of fish bait or worm added to the hook, which renders them useless.

Multiple hook rigs are useful at times — for example in bream, whiting, pouting and haddock fishing — but the hunter with only specimen fish in mind usually puts his faith in a single-hook rig with a correct bait and good presentation. An exception is sandy ground fishing for turbot and plaice. For these much sought after species, it is usual to offer a long flowing trace with a single hook at the end and another placed on a short snood 18 inches farther up. 'Flyer' hooks should never be mounted above conger and ling traces, as used in wreck fishing, or for that matter in any other kind of charter boat operation. They are downright dangerous to a skipper during the gaffing of a large fish and are not allowed by some leading skippers.

Only recently have wreck anglers fished deliberately for turbot. Previously most large ones were caught by accident when a change of tide swung the boat off the centre line of the hulk. Realising this potential, some charter skippers deliberately anchor off the wreck for an hour or so during the slack tide period to give the anglers a real chance of picking up an outsize 'flattie'. There is no season for turbot at wreck marks. Once in residence the fish stays throughout the year and is just as likely to be caught in the depths of winter as in the summer, although records show the greatest number are taken between June and November.

Fishing for turbot on great banks of sand is something every angler can enjoy. Most open-ground turbot are caught between 3 and 6 miles off the land, but there are exceptions and the possibility of a very large fish taking a bait dropped on a shaley bottom in shallow water should never be discounted. The best chance comes on the great banks of sand in the English Channel, such as the Shambles, Varne and Skerries which are swept by a fast run of tide. Between them these banks have produced more big turbot than all other places put together. Their principle food source on the banks is sandeel. The eel is a fast mover but no match for the lightning reactions of a lurking turbot which can rise many feet off the bottom, grab the luckless fish with a huge hinged mouth and bury itself in the shingle again all in a matter of seconds.

The turbot is not given to dashing about in search of a meal. Instead, it lies buried in the sand with just the eyes showing, waiting for the tide to bring food within range.

Pinpointing the banks is quite easy as they deflect the running tide to the surface. In spring tide periods, when the moon is full or new, the water can move very fast indeed and large whirlpools form in some places. For this reason a great deal of turbot fishing over sandbanks is done on the drift, which allows the maximum amount of ground to be covered.

The drift is usually begun a good half-mile uptide of the bank to be fished and the long trace is well weighted to keep the bait close to the bottom. This is most important should the bait bounce from the top of a bank and land some feet behind as it will have missed the attention of the 'flattie' possibly hiding at its base. There are no half-measures in the way a turbot hits the bait. A solid thump on the rod tip is instantly followed by the rod taking on a full curve as the turbot feels the hook, and immediately takes off across the bottom. It will use a tide run to great advantage by putting its tail down and arching the body. This puts a tremendous strain on the line, rod and angler, which often gives rise to the feeling that the hooked fish is enormous when, in fact, it could possibly weigh no more than 10 lb.

It is a mistake to bait small for turbot, which is a species with a big appetite and a mouth to match. So offer a side of mackerel, a generous helping of squid or a livebait such as a pouting, which is hooked through the body a few inches from the tail. Turbot are also very partial to small flatfish, which have proved devastating baits on more than one occasion.

During neap and middle range tides it is customary for most offshore fishing to be done with the boat at anchor. The greatest concentration of fish are usually on reefs behind thrusting pinnacles of rock when the tide is fast, so it is desirable for baited hooks to drop down the side of the wall.

This is where a graph-type sounder is invaluable as it clearly shows the configuration of the bottom. Once the position of a chosen pinnacle is established, and the strength of the tidal run and direction gauged accurately, the boat is taken well uptide before the anchor is dropped. It is a big mistake to anchor a boat on a short rope when there is a fair rise and fall in the water. The action on the steep angle of the warp will break it out very quickly. It can take all of 20 minutes to pull in the rope and start again, which is time that could have been used more profitably in positive fishing. Anchored correctly, the boat will end up far enough away from the pinnacle to allow the lines to drift back with the tide and finish up in exactly the right place. A selection of different size weights should be available.

Techniques for the actual hooking of a fish are varied. Bottom fishing for black and red bream, whiting, pouting, haddock, and to a lesser extent cod and ling, demand a swift strike the instant that a bite is felt. This means the rod must be held at all times. Resting it against the gunwale will never get the best results when fishing for these species.

The conger is the complete opposite. Very big ones will play around with a bait for a considerable time before deciding to swallow it. This does not apply so rigidly to wreck fish; here the population can run into many hundreds and the competition for food is naturally much greater.

A good method with conger is to retrieve line slowly after a fish has been toying with the bait. No attempt is made to drive the hook home until the weight of the fish is felt on the rod tip. After it is hooked the conger will make every effort to return to its lair, or to get its tail around some object. If it succeeds in this, it is very difficult and often quite impossible to make it let go. For this reason the fish must be held tightly at this time and every effort made to draw it away from the danger zone of the bottom as quickly as possible.

Once in clear water the conger should be played gently but firmly through the slipping clutch of the reel. In the case of a big one the worst thing to do is bring it to the gaff quickly when still full of fight. It is at this point that it can very easily be lost.

All fish, big and small, should be 'pumped' to the surface and not physically winched in with the reel. Pumping is simply lifting the fish with the rod and then retrieving the slack line as the tip is lowered to the water. It is the only way of getting a large specimen to the surface if a high-geared multiplier is being used.

Far too much emphasis is placed on a gaff as a means of getting a fish aboard the boat. The only species that demand a gaff are conger, common skate, halibut and shark. Beyond those, all others can be got aboard with a wide-mouthed net. Specialists who fish from private boats often have nets with a 4 ft-wide mouth and a cavernous body which safely secures the largest fish without damaging it. A gaff is a clumsy tool which loses more fish than it brings aboard.

Going it alone

Ownership of a small but well-founded dinghy fitted with a reliable outboard motor opens the door to a new world of boat fishing. Ideally, the craft should not be less than 10 ft in length and not more than 13 ft if it is to be trailed easily behind a car.

Boats of this size can be launched and retrieved single-handed. Anything larger is very much a two-man operation. A trailed boat gives independence and an opportunity to fish tidal rivers and estuaries where a wealth of good sport is to be found. At many places there are concrete hard-standings and launching ramps often close to a car-park, where a car can be left safely for the day once the boat has been launched.

Unfortunately, there are far too many accidents arising from dinghy fishing. Investigation of many tragedies has revealed a pattern of sheer stupidity and a woeful lack of safety equipment. Even though the intention may be only to fish in relatively shallow and apparently sheltered water, the boat must be fitted with a full range of commonsense items and safety aids.

An anchor connected to a fathom of light chain and at least ten fathoms of good quality rope is vitally important, plus two balers, a pair of oars and rowlocks, which are securely tied in position. The outboard should be well-maintained and overhauled professionally at least once a year. Pull cords on models which have a concealed cowling must be given frequent checks for any signs of fraying or wear in the starting mechanism.

A sealed waterproof packet of hand flares should always be carried. Ships chandlers have a wide choice at reasonable cost. A life-jacket should be worn at all times. There is nothing unmanly about it, just sound commonsense. It is asking for trouble to fish from a small dinghy standing up, especially if there are several people aboard; fish can be played and netted quite easily from a sitting position.

Before setting off on an expedition, even in a tidal river, it is wise to take full account of the existing weather and its future condition. A wind-on-tide situation, when the water is running in an opposite direction to the way the wind is blowing, can raise a pretty nasty chop, which is potentially hazardous.

There are many places where dinghies

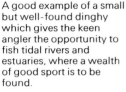

A good example of a small but well-found dinghy which gives the keen angler the opportunity to fish tidal rivers and estuaries, where a wealth of good sport is to be found.

powered by outboard and inboard motors can be hired by the hour or for longer periods. Competitive weekly rates are available in some places, which is ideal for a family fishing holiday. Boat hirers often have cottages or flats for rent within a stone's throw of the moorings. What could be better than being afloat on a picturesque estuary just after dawn on a summer morning, in pursuit of bass, mackerel and pollack? Fillets taken from fish no more than two hours out of the water taste mighty good for breakfast. Hire craft have all the basic equipment with the exception of flares.

The tackle for estuary and tidal river fishing is detailed in the summary of recommended outfits.

A 20 lb turbot is landed with a gaff from over a wreck. These large flatfish are not fierce fighters but they can put a steady strain on the line, rod and angler which creates the impression that the hooked fish is enormous.

Know your sea fish

Britain has a more extensive range of sea fish than many other countries because of its position on the coast of western Europe. Warm ocean currents sweep in from the tropical Atlantic raising the sea temperature significantly and attracting such fish as sea bream, turbot, conger and sharks off our coasts. Arctic species like cod, coalfish and haddock also occur, most commonly in winter.

The majority of the 40 or so common species found off our coasts are relatively easy to identify but some give trouble especially the rays, some dogfishes, and grey mullets. The most important point to remember in attempting to identify a fish is to keep an open mind. This way you will avoid disappointment when you have the identity verified. It is important to check *all* the features given because very few sea fish are recognizable from a single feature.

If you are in any doubt about the identity of a fish — especially if you think it may be a record — take plenty of photographs. Place the fish on the deck or beach, do not hold it in your hands, or your fingers are bound to obscure the one vital feature that is needed for proof of identity.

Bass

This species is at the northward extremity of its range in UK waters and is uncommon on our northern and north-eastern coasts. In the southern North Sea it is mainly a

The British record bass of 18 lb 6 oz taken from the famous Eddystone Reef.

summertime migrant from the south. Found both on offshore reefs and along the coast as adults, the young are attracted to estuaries and are found in virtually fresh water. Grows to a weight of 7-9 lb but due to heavy fishing, specimens of this size have become less common.

Identification: greeny-grey on the back, brilliant silvery flanks. Two dorsal fins sep-arated by a short space, the first fin spiny with eight to nine spines. Two flat spines on the upper side of the gill cover; the angle of the preoperculum serrated with several forward pointing spikes along its lower edge.

● British records: 18 lb 6 oz (*boat*) and 18 lb 2 oz (*shore*).

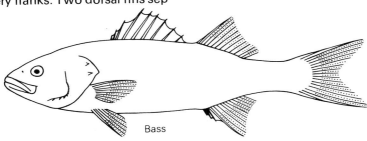
Bass

Red bream

More common on the south and west coasts than elsewhere, possibly due to migration from the south. Most large specimens are caught off Cornwall, Devon, southern Ireland and the Channel Islands, but occasional good fish turn up on the western Scottish coast. It grows to a weight of 3-4 lb.

Identification: back reddish brown, sides silvery with a rosy flush, fins reddish; a rounded dusky blotch at the origin of the lateral line behind the gill cover. Sea bream shape, with a large eye (diameter more than snout length); teeth in sides of jaws rounded, in two to three rows.

● British records: 9 lb 8 oz 12 dr (*boat*) and 4 lb 7 oz (*shore*).

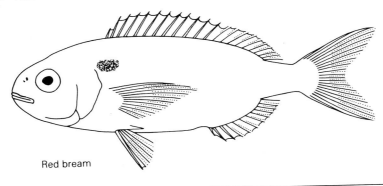
Red bream

Black bream

Best known off the Sussex coast in the Channel but is moderately common all round the British Isles. Prefers rocky out-crops and wrecks. It is migratory although probably only over short distances. Attains a weight of 3-4 lb.

Identification: back greyish, silvery-grey on sides with six to seven dusky vertical bars. A rather deep-bodied sea bream with a small head, small eye, and slightly cur-ved, slender, pointed teeth in the front and sides of the jaw.

● British records: 6 lb 14 oz 4 dr (*boat*) and 4 lb 14 oz 4 dr (*shore*).

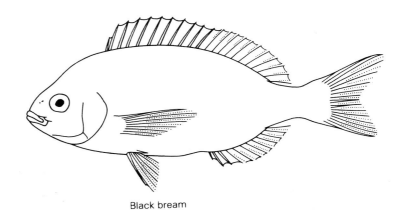
Black bream

Coalfish and pollack

Two closely related members of the cod family which look alike and are often confused. The coalfish also has more common names than most fish — saithe, coley and billet being the most frequent. It is also the pollock in North America.

The coalfish is a more northerly species, found from the Arctic to the Biscay coast of France while the pollack ranges from Norway into the Mediterranean. In general, young fish are found close inshore and the adults in deeper water, the pollack in particular around reefs and wrecks.

The coalfish averages weights of 6-16 lb and the pollack 9-16 lb.

Identification: coalfish — lateral line light coloured, almost straight from head to tail; lower jaw slightly protruding (young fish with a small chin barbel); tail fin slightly forked. Pollack — lateral line dark and strongly curved above the pectoral fin; lower jaw strongly protruding; no chin barbel; tail fin almost square cut.

● British records: coalfish — 33 lb 7 oz
(*boat*) and
18 lb (*shore*);
pollack — 25 lb 12 dr
(*boat*) and 16 lb
(*shore*).

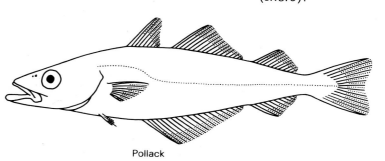
Coalfish

Pollack

Cod

Widely distributed in the North Atlantic, the cod lives from the shoreline down to 109 fathoms although mostly it is the young fish which live close inshore. Migrates southwards in winter so that large cod can be caught close inshore on the southern coasts of England. In deep water it forms schools 5 fathoms and more above the seabed. Good specimens weigh between 10 and 26 lb.

Identification: three dorsal fins, two anal fins; deep body. A long chin barbel, with the lower jaw shorter than the upper jaw. Dorsal and anal fins close together, and the first dorsal with a rounded tip. Background colour variable, greenish or sandy brown with pale mottling on back and sides; white ventrally. Lateral line is pale cream colour.

● British records: 53 lb (*boat*) and
44 lb 8 oz (*shore*).

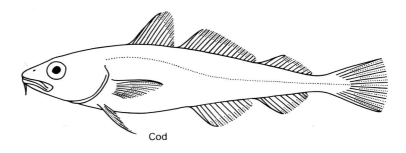
Cod

A magnificent 29½ lb cod.

Conger

Almost at the northern limits of its range in Britain. Exceptionally cold winters may kill many of these large eels. Small specimens occur in shallow water but big fish are usually on offshore reefs, wrecks, and around harbour breakwaters in deep water. Average weights between 10 and 30 lb.

Identification: the only *large* eel found in the sea. Positively identified by upper jaw overhanging the lower. Pectoral fins pointed and dorsal fin origin just above pectoral fin tip. Body is scaleless. Coloration variable, dull brown above, cream or golden brown ventrally.

● British records: 109 lb 6 oz (*boat*) and 67 lb 1 oz (*shore*).

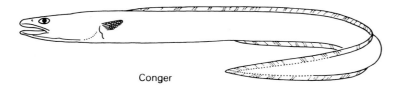

Conger

Dogfishes

A group of five small sharks which have only size in common. The two true dog-fishes are solitary, bottom living species and are closely related. The spurdog is a schooling fish of mid-water while the smooth-hound form small schools and feed on the seabed. (See also Sharks).

Greater-spotted dogfish. Widely distributed along the coasts of Europe. Also known as the nurse hound and bull huss it lives at depths of 1-35 fathoms and usually on rocky or rough grounds. Sexes tend to keep apart except when mating. Adult females migrate inshore in spring and summer to lay eggs. Average weights are around 10 lb.

Identification: a small shark with five gill slits each side, two dorsal fins placed near the tail and a low set tail fin. The second dorsal fin origin is above the middle of the anal fin base. A broad flap over each nostril but the flap does not reach the mouth; the two nostril flaps separate. Usually sandy-dark brown on the back with large rounded black blotches; ventrally creamy white. Colour is not a good identification guide on its own.
● British records: 21 lb 3 oz (*boat*) and
    17 lb 15 oz (*shore*).

Opposite The British record conger of 109 lb 6 oz caught from a wreck on the south coast of England.

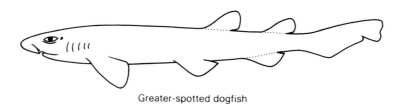
Greater-spotted dogfish

Lesser-spotted dogfish. Often called the sandy dog or just dogfish, this is the more common species which lives in shallower water, although ranging in depth from 2-35 fathoms. It is most common between 2 and 10 fathoms, usually over sandy ground, or gravel, and less common over mud. Females approach the shore to lay their eggs mainly in early summer and can then be caught in shallow water. Average weights are about 2 lb 8 oz.

Identification: a small, rough-skinned shark, with low set tail fin, two dorsals and an anal fin placed towards the tail. The origin of the first dorsal fin is behind the base of the pelvics. A broad flap over each nostril is deep enough to cover the edge of the upper jaw — the flaps are joined together in the mid-line. Coloration: back and sides a warm sandy brown with *small* brown spots; ventrally cream coloured.
● British records: 4 lb 1 oz 13 dr (*boat*)
    and 4 lb 8 oz (*shore*).

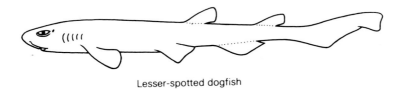
Lesser-spotted dogfish

Spurdog. A common shark which lives in moderately deep water of 5-110 fathoms. Anglers usually catch them in 5-40 fathoms. Typically, it forms large single-sex schools which migrate with regularity, mostly coming into inshore waters in summer. It is most common on soft bottoms, often just above the seabed and at night disperses towards the surface. The females give birth to live young in shallow water. Average weight is between 5 and 10 lb.

Identification: the only common small shark with prominent sharp spines in front of the dorsal fins. Like the other dogfishes it has two dorsal fins, but the first is fairly well forward. Anal fin absent. Body shape slender, streamlined with a pointed snout. Coloration: dark grey above, lighter ventrally; scattered white spots on the back and sides.
- British records: 21 lb 3 oz 7 dr (*boat*) and 16 lb 12 oz 8 dr (*shore*).

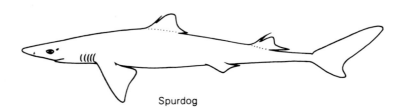

Spurdog

Starry smooth-hound. The more common of the two smooth-hounds in British seas, it is an inshore shark usually found close to the seabed from depths of a few feet to 38 fathoms. Widely distributed in European seas but becomes much less common in Scottish waters. It is particularly common on sandy or gravel bottoms, and pregnant females come into shallow water to give birth to their young, usually in summer. Average weights range between 10 and 15 lb.

Identification: smooth skin (very fine skin teeth). Two large dorsal fins, anal fin present. No spines in front of the dorsals. Teeth in jaws blunt and forming a mosaic-like crushing mill. Grey above and on the upper sides, with variable but usually many small white spots; creamy-white below.
- British records: 28 lb (*boat*) and 23 lb 2 oz (*shore*).

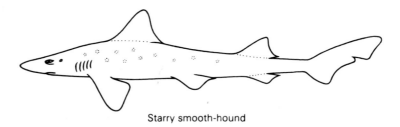

Starry smooth-hound

Flatfishes

A group of fishes which have evolved to exploit the resources of the seabed by going through a process of change during their development at the end of which both eyes are sited on the one side of the head. As a result, the fish lies on its 'blind' side on the seabed. Some groups have both eyes on the left side of the head (turbot and brill), others have them on the right (sole, halibut, flounder, dab and plaice). The flounder is frequently 'reversed' with both eyes on the left side.

Sole. The only common large member of the sole family in Britain. It lives on sandy and muddy grounds in depths of 5-55 fathoms, mostly down to 27 fathoms. Young ones can be caught on the shore. The sole migrates into shallow water in spring to spawn and will often swim near the surface in the tidal flow. Average weights range around 1 lb 8 oz.

Identification: slender-bodied but plump and oval shaped. Head is small and mouth strongly curved. Pectoral fins large both sides. Dorsal fin origin in front of upper eye, joined to tail fin by a membrane. Colouring: warm brown above with dusky patches. Pectoral fin has conspicuous black spot. Blind side white.

● British records: 3 lb 12 oz 4 dr (*boat*) and 5 lb 7 oz 1 dr (*shore*).

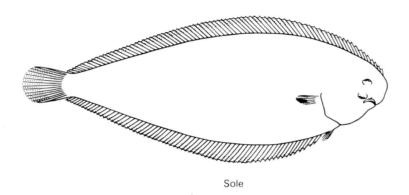

Sole

Turbot. Largest of the shallow-water flatfishes in Britain. Widely distributed in Europe but becomes uncommon to the north of the British Isles. It lives from the shoreline to a depth of about 44 fathoms but only the very young live close inshore. At all ages it prefers sandy, shell-gravel or gravel bottoms, and is more common on offshore banks in appropriate depths than along the coast. Average weights range between 12 and 19 lb.

Identification: broad-bodied and thick-set, the head is large as are the jaws. Both eyes on left side. Body scaleless but with bony tubercles. First few rays of the dorsal fin branched, but the fin membrane runs almost to the ray tips. Coloration matches the seabed, usually sandy brown mottled with dark blotches and smaller speckles extending onto the fins.

● British records: 33 lb 12 oz (*boat*) and 28 lb 8 oz (*shore*).

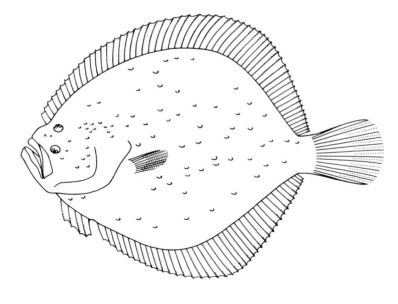

Turbot

Halibut. Largest European flatfish confined to deep water and the Atlantic coast of Britain. It ranges from the south of Britain northwards into the Arctic and westwards to the North American coast. Its depth range is 55-820 fathoms but is occasionally caught in deep gullies at 20 fathoms. Most common on rocks or rough ground. Unlike many flatfishes it hunts extensively in mid-water, well clear of the seabed. Average weights run at about 100 lb.

Identification: rather slender-bodied but deep and with a large head and mouth, with conspicuous teeth. The dorsal fin origin is in front of the upper eye. Both eyes on the right side. Lateral line strongly curved. Skin smooth. Colouring: dull greeny-brown, sometimes almost black. Underside is pearly white.

● British records: 234 lb (*boat*) and 10 lb (*shore* qualifying weight — open for claims).

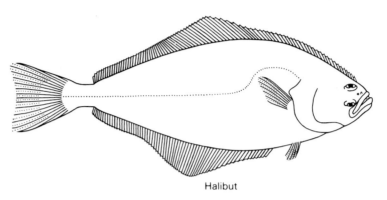

Halibut

Flounder. Common, medium-sized flatfish widely distributed around Europe, from the Arctic to the Black Sea. The only flatfish in Britain which enters rivers and is often found in fresh water. In the sea it is caught from the shoreline to a depth of 30 fathoms but mostly in 1-2 fathoms on muddy or sandy bottoms. It tends to move offshore in winter but this is not a regular migration. Average weights range from $1\frac{1}{2}$-$2\frac{1}{2}$ lb.

Identification: frequently 'reversed' with eyes and colouring on left side of body. Sharp prickles on the bases of the dorsal and anal fins. Some also on the lateral line, otherwise smooth-skinned. Oval body, small head. Coloration: dull brown or greenish brown with darker patches; sometimes orange spotted. Underside white.

● British records: 5 lb 11 oz 8 dr (*boat*) and 5 lb 2 oz (*shore*).

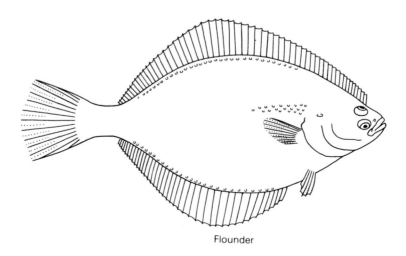

Flounder

Plaice. Found all round the European coastline. Most abundant in depths of 5½-27 fathoms, although the young fish are found in shallower water. Large fish will also come into the tidal zone to feed on cockles and worms and can sometimes be caught in only a few feet of water. It lives on sand or muddy seabeds, occasionally gravel. The adults move into deep water in winter to spawn in early spring. Average weights range from 3-5 lb.

Identification: oval body, small head with a series of bony knobs behind the eyes. Scales are small and skin is smooth to touch. The lateral line is almost straight. Colouring: warm brown with conspicuous orange-red spots, underside a clear white.

● British records: 10 lb 3 oz 8 dr (*boat*) and 8 lb 1 oz 4 dr (*shore*).

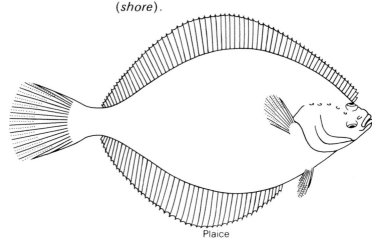
Plaice

Dab. Small and abundant flatfish which does not range further south than Biscay. It lives mainly in depths of 11-22 fathoms. A migration of adult fish inshore takes place in early summer after spawning. Lives on sandy or gravelly bottoms and occasionally on mud. Average weights 1-1 lb 8 oz.

Identification: a small, oval-bodied flatfish with eyes on its right side. The scales on the body are rough-edged, and the coloured side feels rough. A strong curve in the lateral line at the level of the pectoral fin. Colouring: warm sandy-brown, but varying from light grey to grey brown; small dark freckles. Blind side white.

● British records: 2 lb 12 oz 4 dr (*boat*) and 2 lb 9 oz 8 dr (*shore*).

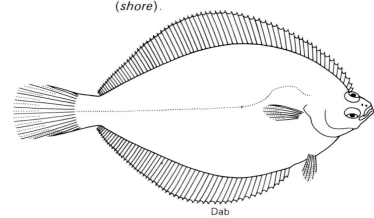
Dab

Haddock

A member of the cod family which is widely distributed in the North Atlantic, both off North America and Europe. In Britain it is more common to the north and is not abundant on southern coasts except in winter. Good specimens come into the Channel from the Atlantic in spring and summer. It is mainly a bottom-living fish found in depths of 22-164 fathoms although young fish can be caught as shallow as 11 fathoms. When very young it floats near the surface under the bell of jellyfishes. Average weight today is only 3-5 lb.

Identification: three dorsal fins, two anal fins and moderate chin barbel typical of the family. First dorsal is high and triangular. Lower jaw is shorter than the upper. Coloration is distinctive: dark greeny-brown on the back, greyish silver on sides; lateral line black. A large rounded black 'thumb-print' above the pectoral fin base.

● British records: 13 lb 11 oz 4 dr (*boat*) and 6 lb 12 oz (*shore*).

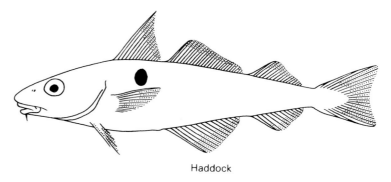
Haddock

A pair of specimen dabs;
the one on the left weighs
2 lb 9½ oz and on the right
2 lb 8 oz.

Ling

Deep-water fish found most commonly in depths of 164-219 fathoms but large numbers can be found in depths of 20-50 fathoms. Most common on rocky grounds at offshore reefs and particularly on sunken wrecks where it often lives in the company of congers. It is chiefly caught in summer and autumn but this is a reflection of better weather conditions for angling than any migration. Average weight between 12 and 25 lb.

Identification: two dorsal fins, the second long and of uniform height; anal fin long. Body eel-like, slender, head large; large chin barbel. Pelvic fins short, do not reach back beyond the pectorals. Dull brownish green, mottled darker on the back, light below. Conspicuous white edges to the second dorsal and anal fins.
● British records: 57 lb 2 oz 8 dr (*boat*)
and 15 lb 5 oz 11 dr (*shore*).

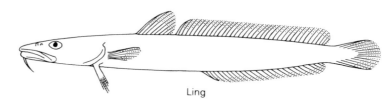

Ling

Mackerel

Widely distributed in the North Atlantic, being found on the North American coast as well as off Europe, including the Mediterranean. It is a schooling fish found close to the surface anywhere over the continental shelf. Highly migratory making inshore movements and northerly migration in spring and summer. In winter the schools move into deeper water and lie quiet near the seabed. Attains an average weight of 1 -1½ lb.

Identification: rather slender-bodied but rounded in cross-section. Two dorsal fins, the first with weak spines and the second followed by a series of small finlets. Similar finlet behind the anal fin. First dorsal fin spines 11 to 13 in number. Coloration distinctive: back and upper sides a beautiful greeny blue with black wavy lines. Lower sides and belly white with pinkish and golden reflections.

● British records: 5 lb 6 oz 8 dr (*boat*) and 4 lb 8 dr (*shore*).

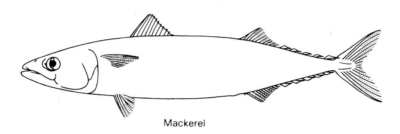

Mackerel

Mullets

Three species of grey mullet occur around the coasts of Britain and, depending on their size, they can be very difficult to tell apart. The thin-lipped and golden are very similar. All the species are streamlined, spindle-shaped fish with broad heads and wide mouths. They have two dorsal fins, the first of which has four strong, slender spines. Their bodies are greeny grey above, white below and the sides have lengthwise grey stripes a scale wide.

Thick-lipped grey mullet. Most common and largest of the grey mullets. Widely distributed in European seas including the Mediterranean. Particularly common inshore in harbour mouths, estuaries and sandy bays. In calm weather can be seen cruising in schools near the surface of the sea. It is also often found around offshore reefs. To a great extent it is migratory moving northwards and inshore in late spring and summer. Average weight of 4 lb.

Identification: upper lip is broad and covered, particularly on its lower edge, with small wart-like papillae. Edge of the lip has fine, closely-packed teeth. Pectoral fin is long and when bent forward reaches the middle of the eye.

● British records: 10 lb 1 oz (*boat*) and 14 lb 2 oz 12 dr (*shore*).

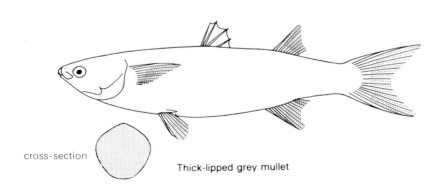

cross-section

Thick-lipped grey mullet

Thin-lipped grey mullet. Moderately common in the south of Britain, but less so to the north, and in Scottish waters with the exception of the Firth of Forth. Strongly migratory, coming into inshore waters in late spring and summer and moving northwards from the western Channel and Biscay. Moves into rivers and is caught far upstream in fresh water. Average weight at 1 lb.

Identification: typical grey mullet shape.

Upper lip is thin and depth less than half the eye diameter. Teeth very fine and close-packed. Pectoral fin short — folded forward it does not reach the eye edge. Anal fin dusky; a black patch at the base of the pectoral fin. Faint golden sheen on the cheeks.

- British records: 2 lb (*boat* qualifying weight — open for claims) and 5 lb 11 oz (*shore*).

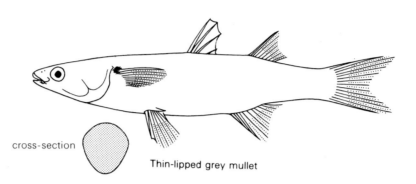

cross-section

Thin-lipped grey mullet

Golden grey mullet. Distinctly the least common of the grey mullets in Britain, but moderately frequent on the south and west coasts. It occurs along sandy bays, in harbour mouths and estuaries but does not penetrate fresh water. Average weight at 1 lb.

Identification: typical grey mullet shaped with a thin upper lip (depth less

than eye width). Teeth on the lip moderately large and well spaced. Pectoral fin, when folded forward, just covers the rear edge of the eye. A conspicuous golden patch on the cheek and gill cover; anal fin light coloured.

- British records: 1 lb 14 oz (*boat*) and 2 lb 10 oz (*shore*).

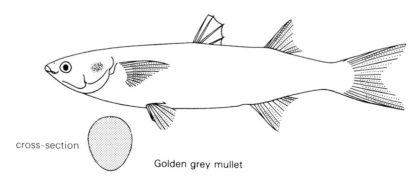

cross-section

Golden grey mullet

Rays

Mostly bottom-living fishes which are relatives of sharks. Like them they have rough skins embedded with skin teeth, a series of five gill slits each side (behind the mouth but on the underside) and a large spiracle, behind the eye, through which they inhale water, while 'breathing'. Their skeletons are wholly cartilaginous. Male rays have a pair of claspers near the vent.

Most rays lay eggs in protective cases but the stingray, eagle ray and electric ray are all live-bearers.

Skate. Largest of the skates in Britain. A deep-water fish found mainly between 49 and 120 fathoms although young skate live in shallower water of around 16 fathoms. It is relatively common on Atlantic coasts and near to deep water and lives close to the seabed, but it forages off the bottom for fishes on which it feeds. Average weight of around 75 lb.

Identification: long-snouted, the front edge of the disc is distinctly concave. A single row of moderately large spines along the mid-line of the disc and tail. Body skin slightly rough ventrally, and on the back (males) or only at the front (females). Dark olive brown above with lighter brown blotches. Ventrally, ash grey or white with lines of black pores.

● British records: 226 lb 8 oz (*boat*) and 100 lb (*shore* qualifying weight — open for claims).

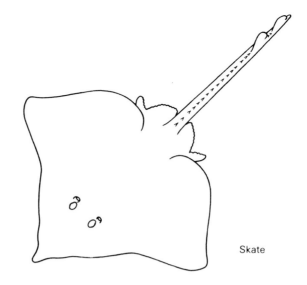

Skate

Bottle-nosed skate. Uncommon skate which is occasionally caught by anglers mainly in the English Channel and off the south-west coast. Ranges south from the British Isles, into the western Mediterranean and southwards to South Africa. Lives in moderately deep water of 22-109 fathoms with the larger specimens usually being found deeper. Average weight is around 20 lb.

Identification: moderately long-snouted, the front edges of the disc are concave but sinuous in outline. A line of spines in the mid-line of the tail with a row on either side. Adults prickly on the back with a bare patch either side on each wing. Smooth ventrally except in the front of the disc. Coloration: pale greyish brown on the back; the underside white with a dusky edge to the disc, black edged in the young.

● British records: 76 lb (*boat*) and 15 lb (*shore* qualifying weight — open for claims).

Bottle-nosed skate

Thornback ray. Most common of the rays in British waters. Inshore species found on muddy, sandy or gravel bottoms, and mainly in depths of $5\frac{1}{2}$-33 fathoms although good specimens can be caught in water as shallow as 2 fathoms. Strongly migratory, large females move into shallow water in spring, and the males follow by mid-summer. Forms loose schools usually of only one sex. Widely distributed in inshore waters and on offshore banks all round European coasts. Average weight of between 5 and 12 lb.

Identification: right-angled corners and a relatively short snout mean that the front edges of the disc are almost straight. The back is heavily prickly and there are several rows of heavy thorns from mid-disc to the tail. Females particularly have scattered heavy-based thorns on the back and underside. Coloration very variable, not a good identification point; warm brown to grey brown with numerous dark spots and lighter patches on the back.

● British records: 38 lb (*boat*) and 21 lb (*shore*).

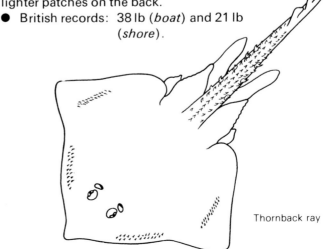

Thornback ray

A fine 16 lb 6 oz thornback ray.

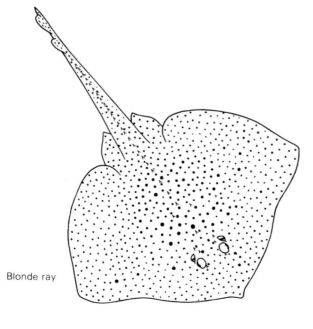

Blonde ray

Blonde ray. Relatively common and fairly large ray which is widely distributed round Britain but is very much less common on the East Coast than elsewhere. Lives in inshore waters, being most abundant around 22 fathoms, although it is captured in depths of 5-55 fathoms. Lives mainly on sandy bottoms. Average weights range from 5-10 lb.

Identification: rather short-snouted and with right-angled corners to the disc, the edges of this fish are almost straight. Adults have a rough surface to the entire back, and have a single series of big spines in the mid-line of the back and tail. Females have an interrupted series of spines on the sides of the tail. Coloration distinctive: the back light brown with a few creamy white blotches and dense dark spots which extend to the very edges of the disc.

● British records: 37 lb 12 oz (*boat*) and 30 lb 4 oz (*shore*).

Spotted ray. A common ray inshore but found in rather deeper water from 14-66 fathoms than either the blonde or the thornback. Most common on sandy bottoms but is occasionally found on rough ground. Widely distributed in European seas, including the Mediterranean, but in Britain it is at the northern-most extremity of its range, and it is least common on the Scottish and East Coast. Average weight is around 4 lb.

Identification: another short-snouted ray with wings that have right-angled corners, and the front edge of the disc almost straight. Fine prickles are confined to the front half of the upper surface of the disc. A row of closely-packed spines runs from just behind the eyes to the dorsal fins. Females and young males have irregular rows each side of the tail. Coloration distinctive: warm brown on the back with dark spots which never reach the rear edges of the disc.
- British records: 6 lb 14 oz (*boat*) and 8 lb 5 oz (*shore*).

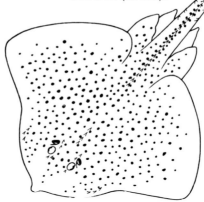

Spotted ray

Small-eyed ray. A shallow-water ray which lives from close inshore down to a depth of about 55 fathoms. Particularly common on sandy grounds, but is localized and is often found on certain favoured sandy bays and outer estuary mouths but not in other nearby areas. Range is confined to Atlantic seaboard of Europe from Northern Ireland and southern Scotland southwards. Average weights fall between 5 and 12 lb.

Identification: a ray with a short snout and rather sharp, pointed angles to its wings. The body has fine prickles on the front half of the disc only, the rear part being smooth. Body and tail with a row of closely packed spines all bent at a right-angle. Coloration distinctive: back greyish to medium brown with large creamy blotches and irregular creamy lines which run roughly parallel to the edges of the wings.
- British records: 16 lb 4 oz (*boat*) and 13 lb 10 oz 3 dr (*shore*).

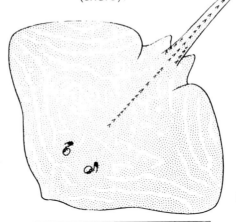

Small-eyed ray

Undulate ray. One of the rarer British rays, its range is such that it is found only on the southern and south-western coasts, southwards into the Mediterranean. Lives mainly on sandy seabeds in depths of 25-55 fathoms, although occasionally it is caught shallower than this. Average weight is around 9 lb.

Identification: a short-snouted ray with rounded corners to the wings. The back is prickly except for the rear edges of the disc and the pelvic fins. A broken row of large spines down the mid-line with odd spines either side. Coloration distinctive: yellowish brown to deep brown on the back with long, wavy dark lines margined with white or yellowish spots making a remarkable pattern.
- British records: 29 lb 6 oz 13 dr (*boat*) and 17 lb 12 oz (*shore*).

Undulate ray

Cuckoo ray. Moderately common ray in the English Channel. Less abundant further north, although caught all along the Atlantic coast. Seems to be absent or very rare in the southern North Sea. Most abundant at depths of 38-55 fathoms, but is commonly captured in depths as shallow as 11 fathoms. Average weight 3 lb.

Identification: a short-snouted ray with rounded corners to its wings. Back is covered with fine prickles, except for a central patch on each wing, and with two rows of curved, closely packed spines, and four rows on the tail. Coloration distinctive: grey brown on the back with lighter patches on the disc and two very distinct black and yellow 'thumb-prints' on the wing centres.
● British records: 5 lb 11 oz (*boat*) and
4 lb 10 oz (*shore*).

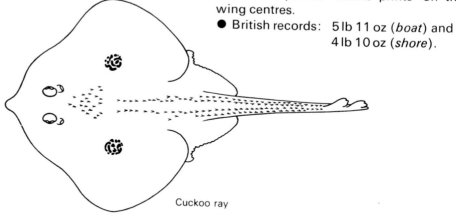
Cuckoo ray

Stingray. Usually found on soft bottoms of sand or mud in depths of 2-40 fathoms. Confined to inshore waters and outer estuaries. Strongly migratory coming into coastal waters in late spring and summer, presumably as a result of a northward movement from the coast of France. Primarily a bottom-living fish, eating shellfish of all kinds, but it can swim in midwater. Average weight between 10 and 30 lb.

Identification: body shape typical of a ray but tail long and whip-like. Lacking a dorsal fin but has one (occasionally two or three) long, serrated-edged spine. *Beware:* these have venom tissue attached and can inflict serious wounds.
● British records: 61 lb 8 oz (*boat*) and
51 lb 4 oz (*shore*).

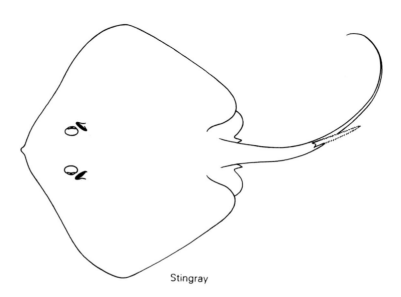
Stingray

Eagle ray. Very uncommon ray in British seas, found during summer and autumn as a result of northward migration from Biscay. Although the eagle ray lives on the seabed where it eats shellfish of all kinds, it is an active mid-water swimmer, usually travelling in small schools. Its migrations occasionally take it as far north as the Scottish coast; mostly it is caught in the English Channel. Average weight about 20 lb.

Identification: distinctive sharp angled wings; the front of the head is distinct from the disc. Tail fin long and whip-like, with a long, serrated-edged, venom-equipped spine (*beware!*) and a small dorsal fin just in front of the spine.

● British records: 52 lb 8 oz (*boat*) and 15 lb (*shore* qualifying weight — open for claims).

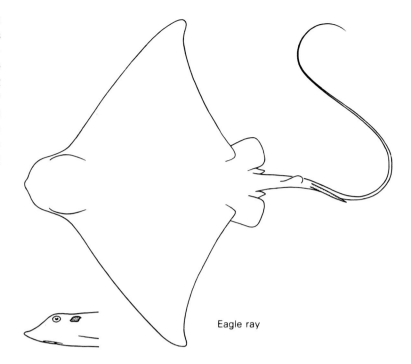

Eagle ray

Electric ray. Uncommon ray on British coast which is caught mainly during summer and autumn, presumably following a northward migration from Biscay coast. It is most common on sand or mud in depths of 5½-82 fathoms. It has been captured all round the British coast but is most common in the south. Average weight about 50 lb.

Identification: when alive gives an electric shock — up to 220 volts at 8 amps for large specimens. Body soft and rubbery; skin smooth. A broad paddle-like tail fin, and two fleshy dorsal fins set on a broad muscular tail. Coloration: plain dark brown or blue, white underneath.

● British records: 96 lb 1 oz (*boat*) and 52 lb 11 oz (*shore*).

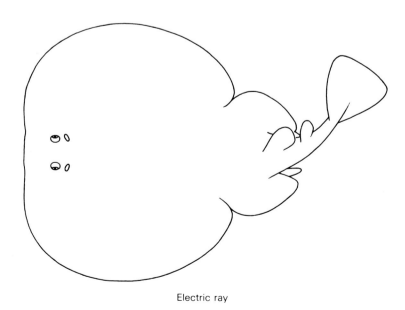

Electric ray

Sharks

One of the two major groups of fishes which have no bones but whose skeleton is composed entirely of cartilage — which may at times be as hard as bone. Sharks lack rays in their fins and have unequal lobes to their tails, the body axis continuing up the upper tail-fin lobe. They have five to seven pairs of gill-slits on the sides of the head (mostly five), and many have a spiracle, a small opening behind the eye. Small shark species are known as dogfishes.

Tope. A small shark which lives in schools often close to the seabed but which also hunts in mid-water. It is usually caught inshore in depths of 5-109 fathoms; small specimens found in shallow water. Strongly migratory and may swim hundreds of miles away. There are also seasonal movements which bring the females close inshore to give birth to their pups. Average weights of between 30 and 45 lb.

Identification: a slender-bodied shark with a rather protuberant snout; moderately large first dorsal fin; second dorsal fin is small and opposite anal fin of similar size. The jaw teeth are triangular, sharply pointed, oblique and serrated on one side in the sides of the mouth. Plain grey in colour.

● British records: 74 lb 11 oz (*boat*) and 54 lb 4 oz (*shore*).

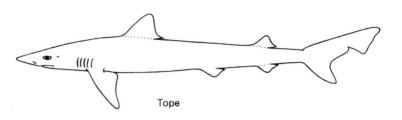

Tope

Mako. One of the few open ocean sharks to occur on our coasts. Cosmopolitan in tropical and sub-tropical oceans, but penetrates into temperate waters, as off Britain, in late summer and autumn with the warming of the sea. Lives in the upper 11 fathoms of the ocean, being rarely found deeper. It occurs only off the western and south-western coast of Britain. Average weight around 200 lb.

Identification: a large shark with a slender body and pointed snout. The first dorsal fin is large; the second is tiny and placed above but in advance of the equally small anal fin. A single keel on the sides of the tail. Teeth long and slender, in the lower jaw hanging forward of the lips; no extra basal cusp. Deep blue or blue-grey above with a sharp transition to clear white below.

● British records: 500 lb (*boat*) and 40 lb (*shore qualifying weight — open for claims*).

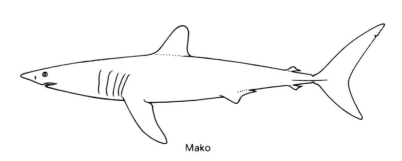

Mako

Mike Millman with a superb 250 lb porbeagle, caught out of a port in the south-west of England.

Porbeagle. Relatively common oceanic shark which occurs all round the coast of Britain although probably absent in the southern North Sea. Found near the surface of the sea, mainly in the upper 10 fathoms of water, but occasionally it is found deeper and closer to the bottom. Although the porbeagle can be caught all year round it seems to be more common in inshore waters in summer, possibly as a result of following migrating schools of prey fish like mackerel. Attains an average weight of about 100 lb.

Identification: rather deep-bodied, plump shark with five large gill-slits. First dorsal fin is high, the second very small and set directly above the anal fin which is equally small. Tail has distinct lateral keel, and a shorter second keel on the lower lobe of the tail fin. Teeth long and pointed, not hanging out of the mouth, a small cusp each side at the base. Deep blue or greyish blue on the back and sides merging gradually into the creamy-coloured belly.

● British records: 465 lb (*boat*) and 40 lb (*shore* qualifying weight — open for claims).

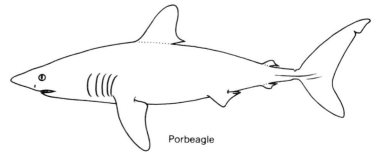

Porbeagle

111

Blue shark. Common migrant into British waters in summer and early autumn. Open sea species living mainly in the upper 20 fathoms of the ocean. With seasonal warming of coastal waters it penetrates into inshore waters and can then be caught in the western Channel, off South Wales, off Ireland, and later in summer off the western coast of Scotland. Makes vast oceanic migrations and sharks in the Channel may winter off the Azores and even further away. Attains average weights of around 75 lb.

Identification: slender-bodied and with a long, sharply-pointed, rather flattened snout. Pectoral fins are very long and curved. Teeth pointed, slightly oblique, with serrated edges. Colouring: back and sides a deep indigo blue. Underside is clear white.

● British records: 218 lb (*boat*) and 40 lb (*shore qualifying weight — open for claims*).

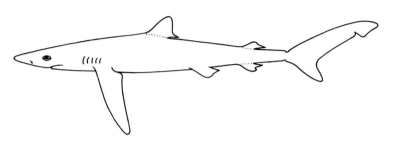

Blue shark

Thresher shark. Surface-living shark which is found mostly offshore, but occasionally comes into inshore waters. Seems rather uncommon in northern European waters, but is found widely in the subtropical Atlantic. Caught most frequently in summer and early autumn, which suggests that like the other large sharks it is migrating from the south into our seas. Average weights seem to be around 120 lb.

Identification: slender-bodied shark with a very short snout, and moderately large first dorsal and pectoral fins. Tail fin is immensely long and is equal to the length of the rest of the body. Colour: grey-blue on the back and sides. White ventrally except for under the snout and the pectoral fins.

● British records: 295 lb (*boat*) and 40 lb (*shore qualifying weight — open for claims*).

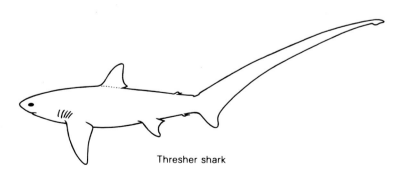

Thresher shark

Whiting and pouting

Both these fish are members of the cod family as the general shape of the tail fin, the three dorsal fins and two anal fins indicate. They are sometimes confused with each other, but this is mainly because some anglers use the name whiting-pout for the pouting. Pouting are also called bib.

The whiting is a common schooling fish in inshore waters. Most abundant over sandy or muddy bottoms in depths of 16-55 fathoms, but is caught frequently much shallower than this. Young fish are particularly common close to the shore, and when very small often float under the bell of jellyfishes.

Pouting also form schools and is caught inshore. Young ones live over sandy bottoms in 1-5 fathoms, larger fish school around reefs and wrecks in deeper water down to 100 fathoms. Largest fish live in the deepest water. Average weights for whiting are 2-3 lb and for pouting around 3 lb.

Identification: whiting — slender-bodied with a narrow, rather pointed head; lower jaw rather shorter than upper.

Young whiting have a minute chin barbel which is lost when adult. Dorsal and anal fins all close together; the first rays of the anal fin beneath the middle of the first dorsal; pelvic fins short, not reaching vent when laid back. Coloration: light, sandy to pale green back, the sides and belly conspicuously white. Black spot at the upper base of the pectoral fin.

Pouting — moderately deep-bodied, with a large, deep and blunt head. Chin barbel long and conspicuous at all ages. Dorsal and anal fins all close together, their bases overlapping. First rays of the anal under the middle of the first dorsal. Pelvic fins long, when laid back reach beyond the anal origin. Coloration: a beautiful coppery brown on the back, yellowish on the sides and white on the belly. Four or five dusky cross bars running across the sides. Dark blotches at the base of the pectoral fin.

● British records: whiting — 6 lb 12 oz (*boat*) and 3 lb 7 oz 6 dr (*shore*); pouting — 5 lb 8 oz (*boat*) and 3 lb 4 oz (*shore*).

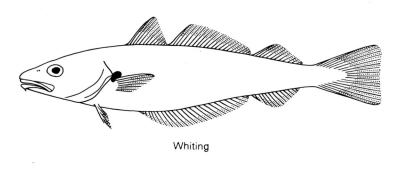

Whiting

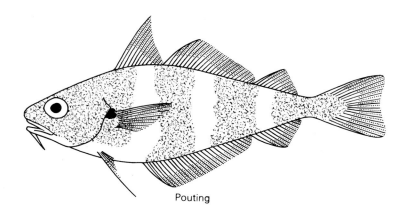

Pouting

Wrasses

A group of mainly small inshore fishes which have fully scaled bodies. Dorsal fin is long with the anterior part spiny. Strong teeth in the jaws and large crushing teeth in the throat – their diets consist mostly of shellfish. Many are brightly coloured and some species, probably most, change sex from female to male as they become older and larger. Only two large species in British waters.

Ballan wrasse. Largest European species of wrasse and probably the most abundant. Common close to rocks and around reefs from about 10 ft to 11 fathoms as an adult, while the very young can be caught in rock pools. Adults form small schools and work over mussel beds on the rocks, swallowing the mussels, shell and all. They also eat crabs. It is almost at the northern edge of its range in Britain and is distinctly more common on the south and west coasts than on the east. It is killed off in large numbers in severe winters. Attains an average weight of $3\frac{1}{2}$-5 lb.

Identification: rather deep body, blunt head and very thick lips, although the mouth is fairly small. Spiny dorsal with 19 to 20 rays in it. Coloration: variable, but large fish green, or greeny-brown, sometimes reddish, speckled all over with white spots.

● British records: 7 lb 13 oz 8 dr (*boat*) and 8 lb 6 oz 6 dr (*shore*).

Opposite A splendid Ballan wrasse caught from a harbour wall in the mouth of a large estuary on the south-west coast of England.

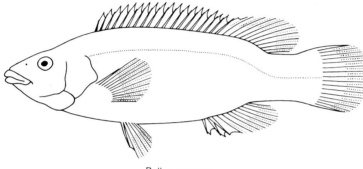

Ballan wrasse

Cuckoo wrasse. Moderately uncommon overall in northern Europe, although in places it is locally common close to rocks in 10-50 fathoms. In summer it migrates inshore and can be caught in as little as $5\frac{1}{2}$ fathoms. An offshore migration takes place in winter. Average weight about 1 lb.

Identification: rather slender-bodied, with a pointed head and thick lips. Mouth is large and extends back almost to the eyes. Spiny dorsal fin with 16 to 18 rays. Coloration: females and young males, yellow to reddish orange on the back and sides, paler on the belly; three large dusky patches on the back near the tail. Males have a blue head, the blue continuing as streaks across the reddish-orange sides.

● British records: 2 lb 8 dr (*boat*) and 1 lb 9 oz 4 dr (*shore*).

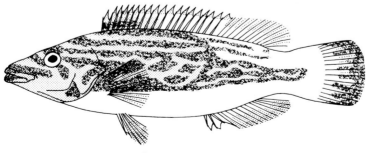

Cuckoo wrasse

Safety

Sea angling might seem a harmless enough sport but it claims unnecessary injuries and lives. Incidents are not limited to boating mishaps — the shore angler faces his share of dangers and, while the unforseen will always take a toll, much of what goes wrong could be avoided.

The most common accident on the shoreline is slipping on wet rocks. It usually means no more than bumps and bruises but can result in broken bones. Slipping usually occurs during walking or casting so make sure the soles of your boots have plenty of grip and select your footholds with care. No matter what the strain, you should always have one hand free to make a grab for something to break your fall.

A positively lethal menace on the beach is a weight that has cracked off during the cast. The velocity is such that it can kill anything in its path. If you cast in an overhead manner then you are unlikely to hit anyone, but once you begin to use sweeping, pendulum-type styles then either a strong main line or a leader must be used.

Loss of life is relatively rare in shore fishing, but on the few occasions it does happen the culprit is usually a heavy sea washing up over piers or rock edges. The best advice in these conditions is simply to stay at home.

Stay alert when fishing flat, sandy beaches because the tide can sweep in behind you unseen, particularly at night or on strange ground. And be wary of mud banks and creeks full of black ooze that could bog you down in a terrifying way. If fog threatens leave the beach at once, for that grey cloak can disorientate you, especially at night.

If you fish from wide expanses of beach such as in estuaries or bays, then a small compass tucked away in the fishing bag is an inexpensive and useful item.

Your tackle can cause injuries, innocent though it seems. There cannot be many sea anglers who have not at some time had the painful experience of a hook stuck in a finger. If the hook penetrates below the barb snip it with pliers on the bend, below the barb, and push the hook through and out of the flesh. Never attempt to rip the hook free. If the hook is impaled deeper than the surface of the skin, seek expert medical help. After removing the hook, the wound must be examined as soon as possible to avoid infection.

Another common, self-inflicted injury is strong line cutting through the skin. This usually happens when anglers try to free snagged gear by gripping the line with bare hands and pulling hard. The line acts like a cheese wire and cuts a painful groove. It is better to wrap the line round a gloved hand or the arm, assuming a thick-sleeved jacket is being worn.

For all these minor injuries it is wise to have a small first-aid kit on hand. All you need are a few plasters and a tube of antiseptic cream — but you should pack up fishing immediately and seek professional help if any injury requires more than this basic first-aid treatment.

Some appalling risks are taken by anglers who go out in small boats in seas that would be hazardous for a 30-ft charter craft. The golden rule on small boat fishing trips is to inform someone of the time you intend returning back to port. When you arrive back on shore telephone that person to say you are safe. If you fail to check in by the appointed time then at least you know somebody will alert the rescue services. Always try to fish in company with another small boat — it is highly comforting in the event of a mishap.

There are seven basic safety aids which should be carried by every small boat.
Oars and rowlocks: make sure they are long enough to propel your boat in an emergency and secure them under seats with cord so they cannot be lost.
Lifejackets: there must be one for every

angler in the boat. Better than lifejackets or buoyancy aids, are flotation suits or jackets with inflatable lungs in the shoulders. Lifejackets are rarely worn — flotation suits, always.

Flares: do not keep them beyond their date and purchase good ones.

Baler: the best is a home-made one cut from a gallon plastic bottle.

Compass: make sure you know how to use it properly.

Torch: for flashing at passing ships should you need help at night, or to guide a rescue craft to you. Keep flashing three dots, three dashes continually.

Spares kit for engine: spare plugs, cloth, tools, sticky tape and soft wire.

Check the weather before you set out by telephoning the local coastguard, who is in the phone book, for an accurate prediction. If he advises not to go, take that advice. He is a professional weather man with knowledge of which winds will turn the local seas nasty. If the weather begins to get lumpy while you are out, do not hesitate to come in. Above all, err on the side of caution and never be pressured into going afloat when deep down you know you should not. You will not enjoy a minute of it.

Glossary

Aberdeen pattern hooks made from tough, springy fine wire, needle sharp with a short barb, equally popular with boat and shore anglers.

Admiralty charts highly accurate charts compiled by the Admiralty's Hydrographic Department. They show the position of prominent landmarks around the coast, sounding lines showing depth of water, comparable perhaps to contour lines of Ordnance Survey maps. Also position of various wrecks, lighthouses, reefs, etc.

Aerated bait bucket the ultimate bait box; contains fresh seawater aerated by a battery-operated aerator. Can keep bait in good condition for extended periods.

Anal fins found below the fish at the rear; can be two separate fins.

Artificial lures these imitate the form of food on which fish are feeding. Modern plastic eels such as the Eddystone eel or Redgill are used to devastating effect over deep-water wrecks.

Bait board a piece of board kept for cutting up bait.

Bait box used to contain livebait, often now made of plastic but traditionally a pitch-lined wooden box.

Bait holder hooks these have a couple of barbs facing up the shank of the hook as an aid to holding the bait in place. Not a popular hook among experts.

Bait needle a long needle, up to 6 inches, used to mount livebaits so that they 'swim' correctly.

Ball sinkers a spherical sinker with a hole pierced through its diameter, maximum size up to 2 oz, threaded on to line for float fishing, trolling, light leger, etc.

Barbel small fleshy projection growing beneath the jaw of certain species of fish, e.g. cod, ling etc.

Barrel sinker same purpose as ball sinker but is a slim barrel shape, up to 8 oz.

Body harness fits around back and over shoulders with clips which hook on to two lugs on the reel. The harness takes the strain from the arms of playing a large fish, allowing stronger back muscles to play a part. Also allows better manipulation of the reel; used in conjunction with a *butt pad*.

Boot grips strap-on metal grips which are fastened to soles of boots when fishing from slippery weed-covered rocks.

Bottom fishing where the bait or lure is presented close to the bottom to tempt the bottom-living (demersal) species of fish.

Box swivels heavy duty type swivels much used in the past for big fish tackle. Most anglers now use a ball bearing swivel for this type of work.

Braided lines Dacron and Terylene are lines with many thin strands braided or woven together; really only suited to fishing the surface layer of the sea, e.g. sharking or trolling.

Breakaway sinkers normal slim pear-shaped sinker with gripping wires protruding which, on commencement of the retrieve, 'breakaway' to trail behind the lead causing no hindrance on retrieve.

Bubble float plastic float which can be part filled with water providing casting weight to deliver a small bait at long range.

Butt pad a belt worn around waist with a cup into which the end of a rod butt can be housed, thus acting as a fulcrum point for the rod when under heavy compression.

Carbon fibre a new space-age material which enables rods to be made with a very small diameter-to-stiffness ratio. Very light in weight but expensive.

Caudal fin tail fin; the shape of this fin is often important in the identification of various species.

Centre-pin reel an old-fashioned reel design where the spool revolves around a central pin. Rarely seen now except for certain specialist applications.

Centrifugal brakes act to govern the speed of the spool on a multiplier helping to prevent over-runs or 'birdnests' of tangled line.

Charter boat in angling terms taken to mean a boat which may be hired for angling purposes, taking anglers offshore to distant wrecks or reefs. Skippered by a professional, often aided by a crewman.

Coastal waters in angling is usually meant

to mean a distance of perhaps up to 5 miles from the shore.

Decca Navigator a sophisticated electronic navigational aid, reputedly accurate to within a few square yards. Receives signals from land-based transmitters and converts them into a numerical read-out which gives the boat's position.

Demersal species fish which inhabit the sea bottom.

Disgorger a small metal rod flattened and formed into a vee to aid the removal of a hook from a fish.

Dorsal fins found on backs of round fish. There can be up to three dorsal fins of two types: spiny, which are hard and very sharp, or articulated, which are soft and more flexible.

Drag system *see* slipping clutch.

Drift fishing when the boat is allowed to drift across a mark under the influence of wind and tide, so covering a large expanse of seabed.

Drift lining a bait hooked with the lightest of hooks and line, then allowed to drift, responding as naturally as possible to undersea eddies and currents.

Echo-sounder a device which emits an electrical signal from a 'transducer' fixed to the keel of the boat. The signal bounces back from the seabed and is converted into a visual display, measuring the depth beneath the keel, and on graph paper shows the shape of the bottom, as well as shoals of fish. Sometimes known as a 'fish finder'.

Elasticated cotton used for tying baits to the hook. Brown coloured cotton can be purchased at most millinery stores.

Eyed hooks have an eye formed at the end of the shank to which the line is tied.

Fathom a unit of length often used in measuring depth. Equal to 6 ft (Imperial) or approximately 2 m (metric).

Feathering a method of catching certain species of fish using a series of feather-adorned hooks on short snoods projecting from a central line. Often used as a method of catching mackerel for bait.

Filleting knife a razor-sharp, narrow-bladed knife used for cleaning and filleting fish.

Fixed-spool reels these are reels where the spool of line lies in the same axis as the rod, the line peeling off the end of the spool. The line is rewound by the bale arm which revolves around the stationary spool. Ungainly in appearance, but highly effective in use.

Flotation suit a one-piece suit, waterproof and windproof, which uses an extremely buoyant material as thermal insulation. Acts as a buoyancy aid if the wearer has the unfortunate experience of falling in the water.

Gaff a steel hook fastened to a 4-5 ft handle, used to lift fish aboard a boat. Best used only for large and lively fish.

Hand flares distress signals which can be held in the hand. Burn with a very bright flame, often emitting a dense cloud of coloured smoke. Other types fire a brightly coloured flare high into the air. Always read the instructions and follow them implicitly during use.

Hollowglass rod a fibreglass fishing rod constructed as a tapering hollow tube, giving a rod which is light in weight with a high degree of strength.

International Game Fish Association (IGFA) an American-based international organisation which exists to promote a sporting ethic in angling. Over the years has established world records for different sporting species in various line breaking strains — hence IGFA 12 lb, IGFA 20 lb class rods, etc.

Landing net a net used to lift fish ashore or aboard a boat. Preferable to a gaff as the fish remains undamaged.

Lateral line found on many species of round fish. An easily-definable line which runs along flanks of fish from head to tail; is believed to be in itself a sensitory organ. Actual shape and position of the lateral line plays an important part in the identification of many species.

Leger leads sinkers intended to hold a bait on the bottom when fishing for bottom-feeding species.

Lever drag a simple system of applying the slipping clutch by moving a lever through a short arc. A movable stop inhibits the amount of movement and thus the amount of clutch pressure which can be applied.

Line backing used on multiplier reels to absorb the enormous compressive force of coils of nylon wound on under pressure. Usually a couple of thin layers of soft rot-proof string is all that is required.

Livebait the use of small fish lightly hooked with a fine wire hook so as not to greatly impede their natural actions. A deadly method for many predatory fish.

Migratory species fish which inhabit our coastal waters only during certain seasons, e.g. bream move south to warmer climes in the cold winter months, returning with the arrival of warmer weather.

Monofilament line a single strand of nylon with a very high strength-to-diameter ratio.

'Mark' a place known for good fishing, often found at sea by lining up conspicuous landmarks or by use of an electronic navigational aid.

Multiplier reels a reel in which one turn of the handle revolves the spool several times, providing a rapid rate of line recovery. A multiplier for boat use would have a sturdy metal spool but a casting multiplier will have a lightweight spool made from a light alloy or plastic.

National Federation of Sea Anglers an organisation which acts on behalf of sea anglers at national level and operates a set of rules to govern competitions etc. Runs a national specimen fish competition to reward a meritorious catch.

Ocean currents movements of vast amounts of oceanic waters, e.g. the Gulf Stream which originates in the Gulf of Mexico, flows up the East Coast of America, then across the Atlantic, keeping the waters around our coast more temperate than they would otherwise be.

Oceanic species fish usually to be found ranging the open ocean.

Offshore reef usually refers to a reef of rock protruding from the seabed several miles from shore.

Ordnance Survey map a highly detailed map showing in precise detail the features of a particular area: footpaths, contour lines, lanes, roads, landmarks etc.

Outboard motor a removable engine that is clamped to the stern of a boat.

Pectoral fins smaller fins, one on either side of the fish, situated just behind the gill covers.

Pelagic species fish which inhabit the upper levels of the sea, generally taken to mean a free-swimming species.

Pierced bullet sinkers *see* ball sinkers.

Pirks heavy chrome-plated or brightly painted metal artificials which sink with a fast fluttering action, provoking an aggressive reaction from the fish.

Plugs these lures often have an articulated body and a diving vane at the head which when retrieved simulates the noise and action of a wounded fish.

'Pumping' accomplished by an angler slowly raising his rod to approximately a 45° angle, then lowering it, reeling in a yard or two of line gained as he does so, repeating the process until the fish surfaces.

Reel fitting *see* winch fitting.

Rod carriers holders which clip into the roof guttering of a car to carry made-up rods.

Rod rest holds the rod steady in an upright position so that bites are clearly visible. Also holds line clear of the first few waves. Usually takes one of two forms: a tripod or a monopod — a single support which is sharp at one end and driven deep into the sand. The rod is then rested against it or on it.

Roller rings line guides originally introduced for use with wire line. They incorporate small rollers over which the wire passes, avoiding any sharp, kink-inducing bend. Rollers should be free-rolling and hardened.

Rotten bottom a length of line deliberately weaker than the main line. The sinker is tied on with this length of weak line so that if the sinker becomes hitched to the seabed the rotten bottom breaks, leaving the main trace and tackle intact.

Rough ground a type of seabed which is usually a mixture of small rocky outcrops, boulders, sand and shale.

Running float generally used to describe any float through which the line runs. Stopped at a preset depth by a short length of elastic band tied onto the line, known as a *float stop*.

Sandeel courge traditionally made from wicker in the shape of an elongated lemon with a little trap door in the top. Allowed to float alongside the shaded side of the boat, permitting free passage of fresh seawater to keep sandeels alive.

'Seamaster' hooks short stubby, hand-forged hooks which are very strong with a tremendous hooking power. Great favourites with conger and shark anglers.

Shock leader short length of heavy monofilament used to take the enormous strain incurred by casting a heavy sinker a long way with a powerful rod.

Slack water the point in time between flood and ebb and ebb and flood when the tide stands still; about an hour on spring tides and up to two hours on small neap tides.

Slipping clutch a clutch device built into most modern fishing reels which can be preset to a certain loading, usually half the breaking strain of the line in use.

Snood *see* trace.

Spade-end hooks these have the end of the shank flattened out. The line is whipped to the shank of the hook. the flattened end preventing the whipping from sliding off the shank.

Specimen hunting an angler who concentrates on catching large fish in preference to a number of smaller fish.

Spinners generic term used to describe a casting lure.

Spigot ferrule used to join two sections of a hollowglass rod. The spigot actually fits into the internal taper of the top half of the rod, giving the appearance and performance of a one-piece rod.

Split shot small spherical lead sinkers fastened to line by closing a split in the sinker which traps the line.

Spoon metal or plastic lure, shaped like the dished part of a household spoon. Often used more as an attractor or lure in sea angling.

Stick float the original West Country mackerel float. Now much used for other sea species.

Storm beach *see* surf beach.

Strike term used to describe the sudden upward and backward movement of the rod to set the hook in the mouth of a fish.

Surf beach beaches which directly face the Atlantic, taking the full brunt of seas which have had no interruption for a thousand miles or more. The wild surf is a favoured haunt of bass.

Swivels generally used as the connector between trace and main line to prevent line twist from travelling up the main line.

Three way swivel a swivel with one eye at right angles to the other two, forming a useful point at which a hook snood may be attached.

Tides an incoming tide is said to be a 'making' or 'flood' tide. An outgoing tide is known as a 'falling' or 'ebb' tide. Flood and ebb tides flow for approximately 6 hours in each direction. A 'spring' tide occurs when the sun and moon 'pull' the tides in the same direction causing the tide to rise and recede further than on a neap tide. A neap tide occurs when the sun pulls in the opposite direction to the moon, so the rise and fall of the neap tide is much smaller than on a spring tide.

Tide tables times of high and low tide vary from place to place around the coast so each area has its own set of tide tables. These often have a set of tidal constants which can be added to or subtracted from times in each locality to find the time of high or low water.

Tournament casting competitive casting where the objective is distance.

Trace length of line to which a hook is connected, generally of a lesser breaking strain than the main line.

Trolling a method of fishing in which a livebait or lure is trailed slowly behind a moving boat.

Uptide fishing a method in which the boat is anchored in shallow water and the baited terminal tackle is cast uptide.

Ventral fins a pair of small fins found just below the gill covers.

Wire booms used in making up various boat fishing rigs. Have the single purpose of preventing the trace from tangling back around the main line as the rig is lowered through the water to fishing depth.

Wire line metal line, in twisted strand or single strand form, made from stainless steel or Monel metal. Used by specialists for fishing areas with a very fierce tidal run where, because of its own weight, the wire tends to 'cut' the water better, so less lead is required on the sinker.

Wire trace short length of wire to which the hook is attached. Used especially for toothy fish such as shark and conger which are often capable of biting through monofilament line.

Winch fitting this fitting holds the reel in place on the rod.

Wreck fishing usually carried out from large well-equipped charter boats in offshore waters. The wrecks are ships which lie sunk in deep water and have become the home of fish. Charter boats usually locate the wrecks by means of a Decca Navigator.

Index

Measurements given in this book are in imperial, but the
metric units can be found by noting the imperial measurements and
using the following conversion table:

Length	Mass
1 inch = 2.54 centimetres	1 ounce = 28.3 grams
1 foot = 30.48 centimetres	1 pound = 0.45 kilograms
1 yard = 91.44 centimetres	

Acknowledgements

Photographs

Angler's Mail: 28, 52, 56; *E. J. Chalker:* 29; *R. S. Coldron:* 76 (bottom);
B. Gledhill: 79 (top), 117 (top); *E. M. Grant:* 37; *J. Holden:* 19, 27, 33,
34, 38, 40, 51, 70, 74; *E. Merrit:* 41; *M. Millman:* 8/9, 30, 31, 35, 39,
54/55, 75, 76 (top), 79 (bottom), 81-83, 86, 87, 90-92, 96, 102, 106,
111, 114, 117 (bottom); *Mitchell Reels:* 20, 21, 57; *I. Muggeridge:* 11;
Penn International: 58; *P. R. Angling Services (P. Peck):* 18; *R. Symons:*
title page, 15; *R. Westwood:* 71.

Line drawings

Peter Stebbing: 93-95, 97-113, 115; *Tony Whieldon:* 23-26, 32, 36, 39, 43,
45-49, 60-66.